Find

G000100038

A

Robin Cooper

with mettā,

Ratnaprabha

Windhorse Publications

Published by
Windhorse Publications
169 Mill Road
Cambridge
CB1 3AN
United Kingdom

info@windhorsepublications.com
www.windhorsepublications.com

First Edition 2012

Typeset and designed by Ben Cracknell Studios
Cover design by Deborah Harward and Marlene Eltschig
Cover image © Zennie
Printed by Bell & Bain Ltd, Glasgow

British Library Cataloguing in Publication Data:
A catalogue record for this book is available from the British Library

ISBN: 978 1 907314 03 2

About the Author

Whilst studying physics and the history of science Robin Cooper discovered Buddhist meditation. He curtailed his career in science to train for ordination into the Triratna Buddhist Order, where he was given the name Ratnaprabha. He is currently director of the West London Buddhist Centre. His previous book was *The Evolving Mind: Buddhism, Biology and Consciousness.*

Contents

List of Figures   vii

Introduction: In the Forests of the Night   1

1   The Windows of Experience   9

2   The Garden of Impressions   23

3   The Mirror of Awareness   37

4   The Rills of Selfishness   53

5   The Lasso of Compassion   65

6   I Am a Miner for a Heart of Gold   75

7   Mind Like the Sky   87

8   The Buddha in the Laboratory   101

Conclusion   119

Notes   125

Recommended Reading   137

Acknowledgements   139

Index   141

List of Figures

1 Buddhist pilgrim (p.3).
2 The Buddha of the *Śūraṅgama Sūtra* (p.16).
3 The eight consciousnesses (p.25).
4 The wheel of life (p.38).
5 Avalokiteśvara, Bodhisattva of compassion (p.67).
6 The five-element stūpa (p.78).
7 The Buddha discovers meditation (p.89).
8 The second ox-herding picture, 'Finding the tracks' (p.123).

All illustrations drawn by Varaprabha, except 4 by Aloka, and 3 by the author, after lecture by Thich Nhat Hanh, 20 August 2006, Plum Village.

Introduction

In the Forests of the Night

The way lies under the foot of every person.[1]

Dōgen

When I was fifteen, one night I turned the radio off in my little bedroom in North London and lay down on the bed staring at the ceiling. 'What is going on?' I thought to myself. 'Here is this living awareness, contained in this one human body that it calls its own, among millions that are mysteriously "other". Why? What's going on?'

The only way I could think of to solve the conundrum of my own subjectivity was to meditate. Goodness knows where I got that idea from, but still I squeezed my eyes closed and waited. But then what? I didn't actually know what meditation was or what to do next. I made a resolution to learn, but the chance didn't come until six years later, under the stress of my university physics finals. The meditation teacher was a Buddhist, and I began my journey of exploring the mystery of awareness using Buddhism. I wanted what I had wanted at fifteen – to explore what it was to be aware. I wanted to find the mind.

Discoveries in the forest

Imagine you are a lone explorer wandering in a dark unknown forest. Making your way uphill to get more of a view, you come across an overgrown road winding through the dense trees. With mounting excitement you hack your way through the brambles and follow the road along a ridge. Some flagstones, a crumbling wall, a ruin, and then, with a gasp, you stumble into a long-abandoned city, with great stone buildings and traces of formal gardens graced by waterways.

The Buddha used this image of a traveller finding a forgotten, overgrown city to describe his wonder at discovering the ancient glory of the human mind, his own mind.[2] The city in its full splendour is the birthright of every human being – it represents a mind fully awakened (Buddha means 'Awakened One'). The Buddha wasn't content to leave the city of the mind in ruins, and he later elaborated his city image to convey what he did with the rest of his life: showing how to restore the city of the mind to its potential glory.

The Buddhist project is simply to expand the scope of your awareness, and to cut through whatever brambles confine it. Buddhists seeks wisdom, which is seeing things as they really are without the veils of mistaken preconceptions and self-centred needs. They also seek love and compassion, which means bringing other people into the sphere of your awareness, and giving them a value equal to yourself. The Buddhist project necessarily has the human mind as its field of work: that neglected city with such a grand future. This book is about finding the mind, finding your own mind. But more than that, it describes Buddhist approaches to restoring the mind to its full potential.

Do you know what your mind is? You and I are in the crumbling, uncared for city of experience that is human life, not even aware of its potential, usually taking it for granted. We'll

Figure 1

come at the mind from different angles: we'll look at awareness, consciousness, perception, subjectivity, and so on, and by the end of the book, we may have a sense of the Buddhist view of the mind.

Buddhism is centred on the mind – on understanding and transforming human experience. But it takes an exploratory approach, it asks us to seek: it is not a revelation of religious truths. The Buddha saw that we are all in a tough predicament, as human beings. We are constantly anxious about what we lack and what we may lose, and in chasing security we easily cause pain to others. But the Buddha did not offer to save us through faith in his truth – instead, he asked us to explore. Be aware, probe the edges of your awareness, explore, and find your mind.

He remembered the time when he was on his own, when he felt as if he was wandering in a dark forest. We are fortunate in that, although we are all explorers of our own experience, the ancient road we can follow has been kept clear by a great succession of insightful people down the ages. So this book too is not a substitute for personal exploration, but a rough guide to finding the mind, informed by Buddhist tradition and practice, especially the practice of meditating in mindfulness.

Attending to experience

> ### *Finding the mind* 1
>
> What happens if you close your eyes for a minute and attend to your experience? I mean a whole minute, not just a couple of seconds – give it time. What you're doing is a miniature meditation.
>
> What did you notice? I'm not going to tell you – how could I know? All sorts of things happen when you attend to your experience. (All sorts of things happen when you don't, but you may miss them.)

At first, meditation is simply attending. But to give meditation a chance of revealing something, even of altering your state of mind, you probably need your mind to quieten down a bit. We lack quietness in two ways – we are busy talking to ourselves, and we are rather bothered. Mental chatter might be planning something, or rehearsing what happened earlier, or perhaps working something out. As for being bothered, probably the most common form nowadays is at least a mild anxiety. But it could also be frustration with things not going right, irritation with somebody, fantasies and hopes for some sort of gratification, excitement, low spirits, or any of a thousand other emotions. With patience and a meditation technique that suits you, these thoughts and emotions can quieten down. Then your experience is less overwhelming, and you've a chance of attending to it.

A lot of us Buddhists have a habit of meditating. So every day I sit down with my eyes closed and do nothing for a while. If I'm not too dopey or agitated, I start to attend. Here is my mind. What happens?

Sometimes I notice little aches and pains, a tension in my stomach, an impulse to fidget. Is it my body trying to distract me? No it isn't: I've found that mind is more complete and more real the more it is embodied, the more it fills my body, so the physical sensations help bring me down to earth.

Sometimes I am more an emotional being than a physical being: I notice excitement, or a longing, or I feel down or irritated, or just full of good cheer. The emotions are in my body too, though generally they set off trains of thought. And sometimes that is what I notice – thinking. Thoughts, usually in words like a busy procession of single-minded ants leaving their nest. Sometimes it's memories and mental images popping up.

Probably something of all these activities is going on while I sit there quietly, and there is another input, too. That is sensory experience: the noise of the water in the central-heating pipes, the weight of my body pressing down on the seat, light filtering between my half-closed eyelids.

If I try and step back from it all, there's an underlying sense of an inside and outside. There is me in here receiving all these impressions – even the thoughts and images seem somehow to be coming *into* my awareness. But is it real, that sense of me inside, peering out? Both thoughts and the sense of being inside looking at an outside do seem to evaporate when you hold them in a steady gaze of awareness. If that enclosed 'me' was something real and solid, would it not become clearer under a steady gaze? As the Zen teacher Charlotte Joko Beck noticed, if the more you look at something the more it isn't there, then you know it's not real.[3] When the more you look at things the more they *are* there (like other people, who stubbornly persist), then you know they *are* real.

So it is in this ever-changing stream of experience that we are going to search for mind. What is it like? How is it structured? What is it capable of?

In chapter 1, 'The Windows of Experience', we shall follow the Buddhist tradition of leaving these questions open as long as possible, so that we can look for our minds without too many preconceptions. Chapter 2, 'The Garden of Impressions', is about the source and destination of the experiences that stream into the mind. Which ones come from within, and which originate in the outer world? How do I perceive things, what effect do they have on me, and where is the 'I' that is having the experience?

In fact, does it matter whether I am really here, watching my experience, or not? Can I look harder, deeper, more objectively, or am I doomed to going round and round in circles, repeating the same mistakes over and over again? That is the topic of chapter 3, 'The Mirror of Awareness', which is centred on the Tibetan wheel of life. Chapter 4, 'The Rills of Selfishness', is about the mind's tendency to home in on a limited part of experience, so that I cause myself a lot of trouble by overidentifying with my body, my preferences, my self-image, or whatever. Then chapter 5, 'The Lasso of Compassion', describes how we can begin to break down self-imposed mental limitations. We can extend our awareness to other people; and being fully aware of another person as a subject like ourselves entails love and compassion.

Compassion is a softening of the edges of our minds. But to what extent can our edges, our limitations be dissolved? In Buddhism there is an architectural symbol of the progressive liberation of the mind – the stūpa, described in chapter 6, 'I Am a Miner for a Heart of Gold'. In chapter 7, 'Mind Like the Sky', we will look at increasingly open mental states, even a mind that is not trapped in the division of inner and outer, and directly knows experience without having to describe it in other people's words.

These seven chapters complete a Buddhist meditation on finding the mind, and in the process liberating it from the straitjacket of its own ignorance. But Buddhists are not the only people to seek the mind and attempt to define what it is like. The great traditions of Western philosophy, and a few decades of remarkable discoveries in the science of the brain, are noble attempts to make sense of the mind. How do their conclusions compare with those of Buddhism? That is the subject of the final chapter, 'The Buddha in the Laboratory'.

But to go back to our central question: what is going on for you now? Who are you?

1

The Windows
of Experience

I am hands
And face
And feet
And things inside of me
That I can't see.

What knows in me?
Is it only something inside
That I can't see?[4]

Laura Riding

The wonder of being aware

Like all children, as I grew up, I picked up ways of describing
my experience. I learnt a great catalogue of things, objects that
I fitted together to build the world I inhabit. I learnt, too, to
recognize other people, and we compared our accounts of the
world. As a result, most of it now seems quite definite and familiar
– maybe a bit *too* definite, a bit *too* familiar. In particular, I learnt to

9

distinguish an outer world that I share with others from an inner world that is mine alone.

It's a puzzle that there should seem to be two kinds of experience, of me, and of what is outside me. Even more puzzling is where I myself am located in this world of mine. Houses and clouds and neighbours are out there, objective. But even 'subjective' experiences seem to impinge on my mind as if they come from outside it, whether a pain in the foot, a memory of a beach in summer, the chatter of my trains of thought, or even my dreams.

It's as if my mind were a window, with two surfaces, one facing outwards and one facing inwards. I can pay attention to the outer world, whatever passes through the outward-facing surface of the glass, or switch my gaze to inner experiences. I like to think that the world outside the window presents itself just exactly as it is, though I'm gradually learning that my account of it is riddled with self-serving assumptions and simplifications. The room on the *inside* of the glass is something I don't often attend to. When I do, it is full of shadows. I tend to assume that 'I' dwell there, even that the room *is* my mind. Yet the inner world is not something I directly experience any more than the outer. All I can be sure of is the window pane itself – my experience – *that* is my mind.

Isn't it wonderful – to find myself here, now, actually aware? What could be more extraordinary? How did it happen? What on earth is going on? And yet we become accustomed to the glow of our own minds, perpetually alight like the Olympic flame. Not only does it seem normal, it can even seem rather stale and limited. Surely it isn't! I'd like to explore how Buddhism tries to open our eyes to the wonder of the human mind that we each possess – that we each *are*.

We can become more aware of our own awareness, the flow of experience that is always changing and so always fresh. 'People travel to wonder at the height of mountains, at the huge waves of the sea, at the long courses of rivers, at the vast compass of the ocean, at the circular motion of the stars; and they pass by themselves without wondering', said St Augustine.[5] And all we have to do to feel that wonder is to be present in the freshness of our shifting experience.

Finding the mind 2

What about now? Is *this* experience something to be wondered at, for you? What is happening at the moment? Try putting down the book and coming into the present.

When I ask you to consider your present experience, you probably focus down on the one aspect of it that seems most significant. For example, you may look around the room, light coming in from outside, the carpet on the floor, someone sitting nearby. Or you may decide: 'What I'm experiencing is the book in my hand, with its black marks somehow turning into half-heard words as they flit in through my eyes.' Or maybe what you focus down on is your body, filled with vitality, tiredness, aches, itches, discomfort, excitement, warmth, and so on. Or your 'inner' self: alert or weary, perhaps a bit bored or uncertain, perhaps serene and comfortable, perhaps in a mood and filled with thoughts of the past and future. Is it wonderful?

For me, more fascinating than the content of my mind is the fact that I am actually *experiencing* it. My mind is illuminated by the light of my awareness. Einstein said: 'Why, if it weren't for this "internal illumination", the world would be nothing but a pile of shit.'[6]

The nature of this illuminated conscious experience is quite marvellous. There is a time when you first notice this as a child or teenager: self-awareness is dawning, and you want to find out what is going on. Can you remember that? Maybe a thought came to you then: 'This is me, this is *now*, how amazing!'

I remember when I was eight, wide-eyed at the green gate to a small London garden, and willing myself to capture the moment. 'This is now', I told myself – 'it will never happen again!' Perhaps a relic of this astonishment at our awareness is what impels so many of us to snap photo after photo on holiday – hoping to tether the flying moment of novelty to something solid and persisting.

For some, the child's astonished vision of the moment returns at special times. An intimate touch can arrest the headlong flight of the present sufficiently for the experience to be richly textured once more, as can the glimpse of a face we once knew, now in its coffin in the chapel of rest. Our experience is only illumined when something removes us from the tunnel of self-concern. Beauty can do it, tragedy, something final, something vast. For a few, most fortunate people, the wonder is there all the time.

The master indicates where to look

Letting self-awareness unfold is what Buddhists attempt, often with the help of a teacher who still cherishes a sense of wonder at his or her own mind, and can look out for potential openings of awareness in the disciple. Then he or she thinks: 'Right, here we go, let's see if they can make use of this!' There is the teenage shepherd boy who meets the sage Milarepa in eleventh-century Tibet, and is sent off to try to answer his own questions about his mind. The very talented boy gets down to his process of introspection, and quickly starts to realize what is really going on. He reports back:

The Windows of Experience

Last night I tried to find out what my mind is and how
it works. I observed it carefully and found that I have
only one mind ... However much one wants to dismiss
it, it will not go away. If one tries to catch it, it cannot
be grasped... If you want it to remain, it will not stay;
if you release it, it will not go. You try to gather it; it
cannot be picked up. You try to see it; it cannot be seen.
If you try to understand it, it cannot be known. If you
think it is an existing entity and cast it off, it will not
leave you. If you think that it is non-existent you feel it
running on. It is something illuminating, aware, wide
awake, yet incomprehensible. In short, it is hard to say
what the mind really is.

Milarepa sends him off again, asking him to investigate what
colour and shape it is, and where it is located.

'Did you try last night to find out what the mind is
like?' The boy replied, 'Yes, I did.' 'What does it look
like?'

'Well, it is limpid, lucid, moving, unpredictable,
and ungraspable. It has no colour or shape. When it
associates with the eyes, it sees; when with the ears,
it hears; when with the nose, it smells; when with the
tongue it tastes and talks; and when with the feet it
walks. If the body is agitated, the mind, too, is stirred.
Normally the mind directs the body; when the body
is in good condition, the mind can command it at will.
But when the body becomes old, decayed, or bereft
the mind will leave it behind without a thought as one
throws away a stone after cleaning oneself. The mind
is very realistic and adaptable. On the other hand,
the body does not remain quiet or submissive, but

13

frequently gives trouble to the mind. It causes suffering and pain until the mind loses its self-control. At night in the state of sleep the mind goes away; it is indeed very busy and hard-working.'[7]

Finding the mind 3

After reading the instructions below, close your eyes and see if you can observe what your mind is like.

Whereabouts is your mind located? What colour or shape is it, and how big? In what way does it change from moment to moment? Can you send your mind away and call it back to you? Can you always freely direct your mind to pay attention to sounds, then to your skin and its sensations, then to your breathing process? Is there silent 'talking' going on in your mind – if so, what about?

After you have explored these questions for at least five minutes, reread the shepherd boy's reports, and see whether or not you agree with him.

The shepherd boy is lucky: he's not starting off with too many assumptions about his mental life. Very quickly he notices that you can't really look at your mind, the subjective side of yourself, as if it were an object, and so you can't answer the kind of questions (shape, location, and so on) that we ask about *things*.

The Buddha himself loved to confront his students with themselves in this sort of way. The *Śūraṅgama Sūtra*, a fairly late Buddhist text known only from China, shows him gently leading his close friend and disciple Ānanda towards a discovery of his own mind.

A monk looks for his mind

Ānanda was the Buddha's youngest cousin, and he became a monk out of his intense admiration for his relative. He followed the Buddha everywhere, becoming his attendant, and he memorized all his teachings in an almost obsessive way. But he neglected his own meditation.

One day, the story goes,[8] Ānanda is begging for food as usual in the town when he is spotted by Mātaṅgī, who has fallen in love with him. She entices him into her bedroom, and he very nearly breaks his vow of chastity. But he suddenly thinks of the Buddha. In horror at his near miss, he hastens back to the Buddha, taking Mātaṅgī with him. Weeping bitterly, he implores: 'I've heard so much of your teaching, yet I am so far from awakening. Today I nearly broke my vows. What can I do?' Ānanda's lapse shocks him into realizing that he is not the master of his own actions.

The Buddha doesn't criticize Ānanda or Mātaṅgī. He just asks Ānanda why it was that he had decided to renounce romantic relationships and become a monastic follower instead. Ānanda replies that he had become a wanderer with the Buddha because he had been so impressed by the Buddha's charisma. The Buddha tells him that the reason people go on and on making mistakes is that they do not know their own minds. He asks Ānanda what it was in him that had been impressed, and Ānanda replies that his eyes saw and his mind admired. The Buddha then starts a long process of questioning, asking Ānanda to find his mind and to understand how he perceives.

'So where is this mind of yours?' 'It's in my body!' 'Well, look around you. What do you see?' 'I see you teaching your disciples in this hall, and through the windows I can see the trees and the river in the park outside.' 'So if you were looking at me through the windows of your eyes, you should be able to

Figure 2

see the inside of your body, in the same way that you can see the inside of this hall. If not your internal organs, at least your skin and hair, the pulsing of your veins, and the activity of your nerves.' 'I can't see the inside of my body, so my mind must be outside my body like a lamp placed outside the room that only illuminates the outside.'

'If your awareness were *outside* your body, then the two would be separate, so when you are conscious of something, your body would not feel it, and when your senses take something in, your mind would not be aware of it.' 'I see what you mean! I've thought it over, and I know where my mind is. It must be hidden in the sense organ, looking out through it like looking through glass.' 'But you can see glass; can you see your eye as you look out through it?' 'No, I can't.'

Ānanda doesn't give up, and the discussion continues through increasingly subtle possibilities for the location of Ānanda's mind. Eventually, the Buddha holds up his arm and forms a fist. 'How do you see that?' 'With my eyes!' 'And what is the mind that perceives it?' There is a pause. Then Ānanda says that through the whole discussion he has been searching for his mind. The perceiving mind must be whatever it is that is searching. Suddenly the Buddha gives a sort of Zen shout: 'Hey! Ānanda, this is *not* your mind!'

Ānanda is very startled, and then breaks down in misery and anxiety: 'If this is not my mind, I haven't got a mind, and I am like earth or a log, for nothing exists beyond what I feel and know. *Why* are you saying that this is not my mind?' The Buddha then patiently tries to point to the deep nature of awareness itself.

Ānanda weeps bitter tears, and at last confesses, 'After I left home to follow you, I left it all to you, and always thought that I could dispense with my own practice, since you would *bestow* realizations upon me. I did not know that you could not do it for me, and so I lost sight of my own fundamental awareness. I realize now that in spite of much listening to the teachings, if I do not practise awareness, I shall come to nothing, as if I had heard nothing, like a hungry man merely speaking of food and never tasting it.'

Observing the observer

The Buddha was asking Ānanda to do something very difficult but absolutely essential. He was asking him to become more aware of his own experience. He was asking him to practise introspection, to look within, but also to realize that whatever he *observed* could not be the mind that was doing the observing. The American psychiatrist Arthur Deikman tried this introspection, and concluded:

> When you introspect you will find that no matter
> what the contents of your mind, the most basic 'I' is
> something different. Every time you try to observe
> the 'I' it takes a jump back with you, remaining out of
> sight. At first you may say, 'When I look inside as you
> suggest, all I find is content of one sort or the other.'
> I reply, 'Who is looking? Is it not you? If that 'I' is a
> content can you describe it? Can you observe it?' The
> core 'I' of subjectivity is different from any content
> because it turns out to be that which witnesses — not
> that which is observed. The 'I' can be experienced, but
> it cannot be 'seen'. 'I' is the observer, the experiencer,
> prior to all conscious content.[9]

However, in deciding that the I can't be observed but can
be 'experienced', perhaps Deikman is less radical than the
sūtra. He needs to look again, and then again. At first, reading
something like the *Śūraṅgama Sūtra*, one is tempted to try to
understand it intellectually, and perhaps find flaws in the
Buddha's explanations. However, it is not really a watertight
philosophical argument, but a description of a spiritual exercise.
The Buddha was talking to Ānanda, but he is also talking to us:
he is saying, 'Notice what is actually going on as you perceive
through your senses and as thoughts or images loom into
your mind.'

Ānanda had been far too caught up in externals. The point
is not really to try to *explain* one's mental experience. The
Buddha as depicted in this story tries to challenge Ānanda's
faith in commonsense understandings of the mind, and turn his
attention away from the ordinary discriminating, thinking mind.
He acknowledges Ānanda's intellectual tendencies, by using
arguments to challenge every definite conclusion he comes to
about his own mind. But he uses more subtle methods as well. At

times he shouts; at times he strokes Ānanda on the head; at times he draws attention to the outer world. After all, it is our awareness of what comes to us through our senses that is our most tangible experience of mind in action.

These are all pointing to one's mind or awareness not as something observable, in fact not as a thing in any sense. Is your mind there to be found at all? Yet experience is all there is; in other words, the mind is all we have. It is filled by everything we view, from things in the park outside to feelings in our guts and ideas in our heads. But when we look for the space in which all this happens, all we can find is more objects to look at. It is so easy to believe that, as we observe things and weave them into the mesh of our explanatory frameworks, we have found the mind. But we haven't. It's as if you find the mind by looking, failing to find, and then looking differently.

Because of his love and reverence for the Buddha, Ānanda brought a natural wonder to his exploration of mind. Yet he still couldn't get the Buddha's point. So eventually, the Buddha went round and asked all the great meditators present to recommend what method of meditation would be best for Ānanda, so that he could break through the obstacles that were keeping him from awakening.

The winning method is ascribed to the disciple known in China as Kuan Yin, who has entered Chinese mythology as the goddess of compassion. She says that the method she used in her own practice was to turn the organ of hearing inwards, and listen. After much meditation, she found that her inner experience and her experience of the outer world merged into one all-embracing awareness. She could fully hear all the events going on in her mind, but she could also, as it were, hear all that was happening in the world. And still Kuan Yin is known as the 'regarder of the cries of the world'. According to the faithful, she listens to the sounds of suffering, and responds to them.

Ānanda was known as a great listener: he memorized everything the Buddha said, but he hadn't realized that he needed to listen to *himself*, and then to listen to those cries of the world. So Ānanda went away and practised this meditation of inner listening.

All Buddhist meditation is, in a sense, inner listening. In its simplest form, meditation means attending with a quiet mind to the whole flux of experience, without grabbing at anything, without pushing anything away, and without falling into habitual preconceived notions about what is happening. Unless your mind is already very quiet, it's best to direct your attention at first to something specific. This needs to be something that will tend both to calm the mind and to purify your emotional state; two among many possibilities are the sensations of breathing, and thoughts of goodwill towards other people. You find your mind by paying attention, and it is possible to do this under any circumstances. But when it goes well, meditation is something special, because your mind can be still and clear, deeply attending within an unobstructed space.

Ānanda dutifully applied himself to his meditation. His progress was slow, and he was still striving after the Buddha had died. The other monks nagged him: 'You've memorized all the Buddha's teachings. We need your help to establish what the authentic Buddhist tradition is. We can't wait forever for you to gain awakening so that you have an inner touchstone of truth, and can be sure you have remembered the teachings accurately. Come on, get on with it!'

He screwed up his eyes and tried and tried the meditation of inner listening. After many hours he gave up. He let go, and in exasperation leapt into his bed to go to sleep. But in the air (the story goes), after his feet had left the ground and before his body touched the mattress, he was awakened; he had his great realization of the true nature of mind.[10]

Its nature was *this* experience, in this present moment. Can you notice it? Can you expand your perspective beyond its narrow focus, taking it all in, allowing it all to be as it is, whether beautiful or ugly, whether welcoming or threatening, and just notice how unique it all is? This is the first time anything has ever been like this! All of it, here it is. It is inner ... it is outer, but you don't worry too much about where the boundary lies.

In the next chapter we'll see how that boundary is more like an arbitrary line drawn on a map than an insurmountable barrier.

2

The Garden
of Impressions

'The little soul wavers away', wrote the Emperor Hadrian.
How irretrievably unjust that yours, stored with its singular
cargo, should break up forever. Or is it the puzzling ship
of Theseus that every sleep pulls apart to its least peg and
every waking rebuilds with new matter in the old form so
that there is no I to your I, no continuing self, but successive
semblances that fade and wear out at last?[11]

Robert Kaplan

Seeds in the substrate

In the quest to find your mind, perhaps it's enough to look for
it, to fail to find it, and to keep looking in different ways until
your preconceptions are discarded and some new perspective
emerges. Perhaps you should put down this book and close your
eyes – *this* is real experience, now, here. Buddhism has always
encouraged this real and personal quest. But Buddhist teachers
have also published a stack of maps and guidebooks that describe

the mental landscapes we all have in common, marking the safe routes. So I shall continue with this book, sketching in an account of the Buddhist geography of the human mind, and I hope you will want to stay with me.

As we wander through the forests of our lives, we don't realize that from every act a seed is liberated. Like a dandelion seed in a meadow, it drifts down and lodges in the soil of the depths of our minds. The Buddha uses this image. He says that, as a viable seed in good moist soil will sprout and grow, the same will happen with any action: 'wherever one's selfhood turns up, there that action will ripen. Where that action ripens, there one will experience its fruit.'[12] For example, suppose you disparaged your child's first drawing when she brought it home from school, and failed to notice her distress. Those words do not vanish: Buddhism says they are like seeds dropped into the mind's depths, and one day their fruits will return to sour your future, though you can ameliorate that sourness with kinder actions. A parent's neglect is a strong example, but even the tiniest selfish seeds have their sprouting, according to the karma idea. The karmic seeds might not even yield fruit until a future life – see the box on rebirth at the end of this chapter.

Later Buddhist teachers developed the Buddha's image into a model: there is a substrate (*ālaya*) to consciousness, a soil in which the seeds of acts are embedded, to sprout as life experiences when the conditions are right. An 'act' (*karma*) means anything we initiate, whether a thought, a few casual words to someone, or a deed. They all have their effects, and the intentional ones change our character and thus our future most powerfully of all. Every experience we encounter also scatters seeds into that soil.[13]

This is the model of the substrate consciousness. It is like a vast fertile land, in which lie sprinkled the seeds of all past actions and experiences. Stalking about in that land, the substrate, is the 'small mind',[14] technically the 'tainted thinking consciousness', a twisted way we have of responding to experience. Our personal small mind

24

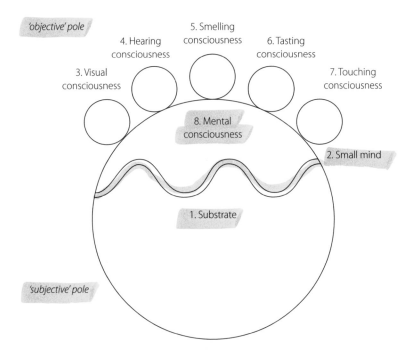

Figure 3 Diagram of the eight consciousnesses

walls off a parcel of land, and defends it as a garden of its own. The small mind is obsessed by what grows in its garden, and it gazes suspiciously over the wall, trying to make sense of all that it sees.

For Buddhism, awareness is the natural function of the human mind. But ignorance taints or defiles that awareness, hemming it in, and the resulting small mind is highly proprietorial over a small patch of what awareness notices, a patch (the walled garden of my image) that seems to be 'oneself'. The small mind is convinced that there are inside experiences that come from within its jurisdiction, and outer experiences that come over the wall, through the chinks of the five senses, from the world outside.

So the model of substrate consciousness ends up with eight or even nine consciousnesses. There is the substrate itself (the *ālaya*); then the small mind; then the model distinguishes a consciousness for each of the five senses (awareness of sights, sounds, smells, and so on); and finally a mental consciousness, which is aware, like a sixth sense consciousness, of thoughts, images, memories, and so on, and also marshals what's in the other five sense consciousnesses.

Figure 3 shows the five sense consciousnesses at the top. They are prodded by stimuli from the senses, and send their messages into the mental consciousness, which tries to make sense of them. The mental consciousness also receives thoughts, memories, and so on from the substrate, but they come in through the distorting intermediary of the small mind.

The consciousnesses

1. Substrate consciousness (*ālaya*)
2. Tainted thinking consciousness (small mind)
3. Visual consciousness
4. Hearing consciousness
5. Smelling consciousness
6. Tasting consciousness
7. Touching consciousness
8. Mental consciousness

The inner and outer worlds

According to the substrate model, all we perceive is mental impressions. Our division of these impressions into perceptions of objects in an outer world and mental activity from an inner world is a subsequent overlay, and it doesn't necessarily reflect the way things really are. This is rather a disturbing idea, but let us stay with it for a while. What we've got is a perceptual situation, which has two poles to it. At one end is what we regard as the subjective content of the situation – 'myself' and everything I think of as mine. At the other end is everything and everyone that is (as I started to discover when I was a baby) outside of my control – the objective content of the situation.[15]

Then the substrate is the potentially undifferentiated material of awareness, which has been polarized by the small mind into an inside and an outside, or even into mind and matter, the two poles of one perceptual situation. Some things seem obviously to belong, without question, to one pole or the other. But if you're prepared to challenge the split just a little, then why not try to work out exactly where the boundary is? A friend you meet in a dream – is she outside or inside? A horse you see on the horizon at dusk – is it really outside if later it turns out to have been only a bush? Your sense that the day is going really badly – is this day, a sequence of experiences, something within or not?

I should say that most Buddhist traditions don't deny that there is a real 'objective' world, including other people, and none of them say that the world is really just a figment of one's own personal consciousness. But when we describe our world, when we respond to it, we are almost certainly describing a construction within our mind separated by several gauzy curtains (preconceptions, desires, and fears) from whatever 'real' world blithely proceeds without us.

Consciousness itself can't be observed. Yet consciousness exists, here it is. And there is no consciousness, no awareness, says Buddhism, without an object. All that can be present in awareness is the apparent object or objects of awareness – you can't look back at your awareness. Speaking of awareness or consciousness and its objects seems to divide the world into two great segments, but that is only a function of language. All we have access to are those 'objects' that are illuminated by awareness; some of them are mental, such as images, others sensory.

This is an ancient account, from the *Laṅkāvatāra Sūtra*, an important source for the substrate model:

- there is an unending succession of sense-concepts flowing into this discriminating or thinking [small] mind...
- which combines them and discriminates them...
- and passes judgement upon them as to their goodness or badness.
- Then follows aversion to or desire for them...
- and attachment...
- and deed...
- thus the entire system moves on continuously and closely bound together.
- But it fails to see and understand that what it sees and discriminates and grasps is only a manifestation of its own activity and has no other basis...
- and so the [small] mind goes on erroneously perceiving and discriminating differences of forms and qualities...
- not remaining still even for a minute.[16]

The small mind 'interprets the impressions it receives from the other six [consciousnesses] as representing an objectively existing external world, and at the same time interprets a reflection in itself of the [substrate consciousness] in terms of a separate, real self'.[17]

Looking for a Self

A separate, independent self, then, is no more than an interpretation. Buddhism predicts that, when I look for the 'I' that half my thoughts refer back to, I won't find anything there.

Concluding that the 'I' is more an idea than a thing, Buddhism agrees with modern brain science, as we will see in chapter 8. But my small mind can't accept that. It teeters on a brink between inner and outer experience. And in the same way that it tries to make sense of outer experience by dividing it up into named things, it also tries to make sense of inner experience by identifying a definite agent, a subject, an independent being who is having all these experiences – the Self.

There is no harm in speaking of 'I' and 'myself' when I'm describing what is coming from the inner pole of my experience. No harm as long as I don't take it too literally. Literalizing one's sense of self leads to all sorts of problems, according to Buddhism. It leads to fixed views of self that undermine one's ability to act, to change, to have confidence. More subtly, it leads to what is called the 'I am conceit',[18] an attachment to the perspective of inner and outer that prevents one from simply taking experience as it is, in a full and lucid awareness with no preconceptions.

It is interesting to catch yourself when you say or think 'I am' – hungry or hopeful, sad or sorry, or any self-limiting adjective. As an experiment, try substituting 'there is' hunger, hope, and so on. The Buddha particularly warned against insisting that 'I am' better, worse, or even the same as other people. Comparisons easily drown out the open possibilities that each experience offers.

Manufacturing a view of who we are, some fixed view of self, takes up a lot of our mental energy. We tend to pursue a tiring semi-conscious narrative concerning what sort of person we are, what we prefer or despise, how we compare with others. But, despite all this effort, there's nothing stable in our inner experience. As the Buddha put it, 'Whatever he conceives (himself as), it becomes different from that.'[19] Only a part of the substrate consciousness is visible to us. And we identify with a *part* of that visible part, and regard it as our self. We are fencing off a small garden in that boundless terrain, the small territory that we identify with.

What precisely we locate inside the fence might alter, but early Buddhist tradition identifies it as belonging to one or more of the five clinging clusters.[20] These are five factors involved in the experiential process, which together can be seen as covering every aspect of any individual living being. It is very instructive for me to notice which of the clusters I hold to most strongly as defining the real me.

The clinging clusters

1. Bodily form
2. Felt responses
3. Perception and recognition
4. Impulses (personality habits)
5. Conscious awareness

If we are the sort of person who is preoccupied with appearance or health, perhaps we identify the self mainly with our body. Or we identify with our felt emotional responses, our preferences, and refuse to have their validity challenged. Or maybe, for us, it is an inner perceiver, taking first watch behind that fence – we insist on knowing what everything is, and where it fits in our life. Alternatively, it may be our complex and deep-seated habitual impulses that make up personality – 'I am impulsive and easily irritated, but quite generous.' Most subtly, we identify with conscious awareness itself.

There are probably more possibilities, and these can be combined; in fact the Buddha suggests that we are prone to several types of self-error within each of these five areas. He says:

> An uninstructed, run-of-the-mill person ... assumes
> form [the body] to be the self, or the self as possessing
> form, or form as *in* the self, or the self as *in* form. He is
> seized with the idea that 'I am form' or 'form is mine.'
> As he is seized with these ideas, his form changes &

alters, and he falls into sorrow, lamentation, pain, distress, & despair over its change & alteration.[21]

The Buddha repeats this for felt responses, perceptions, impulses, and consciousness, as well as one's bodily form. Notice how he is not making a philosophical point, for the sake of argument, about the status of the self: he's pointing out the distress and even despair that comes from identifying strongly with something that is bound to alter.

Ways of identifying

1. It is me.
2. It is mine.
3. It is *in* me.
4. I am *in* it.

So the Buddha pointed to these five 'clinging clusters' as five aspects of the human personality. We tend to grab hold of them as 'I' or 'me' as they circle around consciousness, which is the central cluster. They play an important part in the early Buddhist understanding of how experiences become conscious, an understanding that predates the substrate model, but informs it.

The clusters and perceiving

How does an experience happen? Buddhism attempts to model the processes of perception. Whenever something arises in our awareness, it does so through a sequence of momentary mental states, events that follow on from each other in ways that can be understood, and to some extent even watched, if our mind is sharp enough. An ancient Buddhist commentator imagines a group of poor street urchins playing in the road:

- The process of moments of awareness is like a gang of boys sitting in the road and playing in the dust.
- An object impinging on the sensitive surface of the eye is like a coin thrown that strikes the hand of one of the boys.
- The mind being set in motion is like the startled boy asking: 'What is this?'
- The visual consciousness seeing is like a different boy saying: 'It is something silver-coloured.'
- The resulting receiving state of mind starts as another boy seizes the coin firmly together with some dust.
- Another moment of consciousness investigates the object, like another boy saying: 'It's a round and flat thing.'
- Then recognition comes to a conclusion about what it is and what significance it has, like another boy saying: 'This is a valuable *kahāpaṇa* coin.'
- Finally the recognition of the object leads to impulses to act, like the boys' mother making the coin into some silver jewellery.[22]

The first cluster, the body, includes the physical eye. The coin striking the boy on the hand starts the perception process – it is the eye being stimulated by a visual impression. Then (or simultaneously) there is a cascade of mental events, which includes conscious awareness, the fifth cluster, and perception or recognition, the third. Finally come the volitional actions (included under the fourth cluster) that are set off by the perception: Mum gratefully taking the coin to make jewellery with.

Not mentioned in this account is the second cluster, the felt response, which is the feeling tone that is said to accompany every experience, every moment of consciousness. (Perhaps we could add a boy delighted at the shiny disc.) As a result of our past associations with similar experiences, we are going to find this one pleasant (and so, welcome), unpleasant (and so, unwelcome), or neutral. It seems that we are born with some preferences, and traditional Buddhism would ascribe this fact to experiences in past lives – see the box on rebirth at the end of this chapter.

Consciousness is present throughout, but the pinnacle of the whole process is *knowing*, when all the resources of your mind have done their best to present you with the full significance of the situation for you. That is a culminating momentary consciousness, probably starting off a whole train of thoughts and emotions, in turn interrupted by new stimuli coming in from the senses or from the mind. Pretty much the same process goes on whether the stimulation comes in through one of the physical senses, or whether it's an idea that pops up in the mind, the mental sense.

Remember, each of the senses is said to have its own consciousness associated with it: a distinct consciousness for seeing, for hearing, for smelling, for tasting, for touching, and the last one for the sixth sense, the mind sense. This mind consciousness, as well as receiving ideas, memories, and so on from the substrate, also receives input from each of the other sense consciousnesses. In the analogy, the visual consciousness was the boy who discerned a nameless silver-coloured object. It took another boy, the mind consciousness, further down the chain, to discern the coin in detail, and then it needed the help of the third cluster, recognition (the last boy), to come to a conclusion of what little treasure had fallen into their laps.

It would be neat to see a simple chain of perception running through the five clusters – something like a bodily sensation (1) leading to a rapid feeling-response (2), followed by consciousness of the object (5), then the dawning of recognition (3), and finally getting a volitional response going (4). For example, imagine you see (1) a fast-moving brown shape under the sink – an instinctive alarmed/shrinking feeling (2) – an awareness (5) of that brown movement – realizing it is a mouse (3) – smearing some peanut butter in the humane trap and putting it on the floor (4).

That sequence is part of the picture, but the clusters, as their name implies, are not really discrete separable parts of the human personality, and the mental process is really a torrent of momentary mental events, spinning through contributions from all five clusters, all influencing each other. For example, why is it that one notices (consciousness) some things and not others? And why is it that some things are welcome and some unwelcome (feeling-tone)? The reason is said to be past karma: the decisions we have made, the habits we have entrenched, perhaps in previous lives, in short all our seeds of ethical and unethical actions; these give significance to our current world, and determine what we notice and what we do about it – the fourth cluster.

What happens when I die?

I expect you've heard that rebirth is part of the traditional Buddhist view. Most people tend to one of two extreme views on what happens at death. One is that you survive death, and the other is that you don't survive death. You'd think that one or other of these must be true, but no, says the Buddha. There isn't even a persistent entity, a self, during life, so there is definitely no soul that persists from one life to another. But yet the karmic processes that you have set in motion during your life, those seeds you have sown in the substrate, don't simply vanish at the moment when the body becomes a corpse. Somehow they are still viable; they can germinate and have an influence over another person, newly conceived. More than an influence – the view is that a foetus growing in its mother's womb can't survive without some non-physical contributions from a previous life. So it's

---

not *you* that survives death, yet processes that have built up during your life do go on to have their own consequences in another future life.

The Tibetans take a special interest in what happens to consciousness during dying and rebirth. Some of the features of their accounts agree with modern near-death experiences, and with the accounts of children who say they can remember previous lives. So it could be that texts like the *Tibetan Book of the Dead* are based on genuine memories.[23] Or maybe not.

If your death is not sudden, they say, your awareness gradually withdraws from the senses one by one, hearing being the last to go. Your breathing stops, your heart stops, and your body becomes colder and colder. You may then have some sort of out-of-body experience, where you seem to be witnessing what's happening to your dead body, including the peculiar responses of your relatives. Then ordinary awareness is lost, you fall into a deep swoon. After some time, a rather different kind of after-death awareness gradually emerges, starting with the dazzling lights of reality, either white or coloured.

The lights elaborate into complex hallucinatory visions, like a stream of dream experiences, including benign and angry 'Buddhas' (which one tends to shrink from unless one has a great depth of spiritual experience), and comforting images of various situations, or worlds. For a while you wander in a mind-made body through the landscapes of death. You feel most at home in one of the worlds, because the seeds of actions (karma) that you have accumulated suit you to that world. It feels like home, even if it is very unsatisfactory! So you zero in on a couple making love, say the rather lurid Tibetan accounts, then you sulkily squeeze yourself in between them, and go into another swoon as your consciousness and the other clusters of your personality hastily gather around the newly conceived embryo.

Carrying seeds from a previous life means that the child starts off to some extent with his or her own personality, with preferences, and perhaps with a disposition to be cheerful or moody, gregarious or solitary. It certainly doesn't start off with the consciousness of an elderly adult, and it needs to begin afresh with gathering life experience. Some of the challenges it has to face may be constructed by karma, which guided it to that familiar territory it felt secure in before birth, but the popular idea that every talent or disability is due to previous life actions (karmas) is not correct: the Buddha rejected the view that all you experience is determined by your past actions. He explicitly stated that there are several strands of causation; karma is only one of them. The environment is another, so are factors influencing health, and there are several more.[24]

You don't have to believe in rebirth to be a Buddhist, but it has been a pretty universal Buddhist viewpoint, and the Buddha argued against the materialist view, prevalent among scientifically minded people today, that consciousness is merely something produced by the physical body. No, he said, the body and consciousness are closely involved with each other, yet the momentum of consciousness pushes through the barrier of death. However, there is nothing that is reborn, no enduring substance, no Soul.

At the start, consciousness in the embryo is dim and rudimentary. Gradually it becomes sharper in the womb, and awareness grows in scope, step by step, after the baby is born. Now grown up, we have a mature consciousness. Or do we? What does it mean to be conscious and aware, and does awareness sit at a stable, even level? Let's start a new chapter.

3

The Mirror
of Awareness

*Every life is many days, day after day. We walk through
ourselves, meeting robbers, ghosts, giants, old men, young
men, wives, widows, brothers-in-love. But always meeting
ourselves.*[25]

James Joyce

*With what reluctance do we look into the glass, after rising
from a sick-bed! The recovery we feel: the effects of past
diseases are all we see.*[26]

Goethe

The wheel of life

Early on in my exploration of meditation, I decided I would rent
somewhere quiet for a week or two, and have a solitary retreat.
I found a little stone cottage in the Yorkshire Dales and devoted
myself to meditating (when I wasn't watching snooker on the
television). To inspire me, I took along a taped lecture on the

Figure 4

Tibetan wheel of life.[27] The wheel of life is depicted as a large disc full of pictures in concentric circles – an early graphic novel – displayed to us by a leering demon, the Lord of Death. The lecture explained that what the demon really holds up is a mirror, the same one that he shows in Buddhist myth to the newly dead. Our task is to look unflinchingly into that mirror, seeing ourselves as we are, and not as we would like to be.

With a shock, the first true reflection we see in the mirror is our natural substructure, our animal drives, shown in the innermost circle as a pigeon or rooster, a snake, and a pig, chasing each other's tails. The pigeon represents craving, the snake hatred, and the pig illustrates wilful ignorance. Now, I listened to the tape in short chunks, wandering around the house as it played, and it dawned on me that the little cottage was full of mirrors. As I remember it, there were thirteen of them! Everywhere I turned, I saw my own face looking back at me, as if the demon was there, not letting me get away from myself. I stared into one of the mirrors, and saw myself gradually becoming more like my father; perhaps that perception hinted at my family tree, vanishing into the distant past, leaving lingering animal drives as my fundamental motivations.

Reflexive consciousness and mindfulness

The demon's mirror is self-awareness. It is for looking not at your face, but at your mind, your consciousness. Some people *equate* consciousness with self-awareness, and so say that animals are not conscious. But animals are clearly alert and aware of what they sense. What nearly all of them lack is *reflexive* consciousness – the ability to observe their own mental processes as well as their sensed world. (This must be closely connected with their lack of conceptual language. Bertrand Russell remarked: 'However eloquently [a dog] may bark, he cannot tell you that his parents were honest but poor.')[28] We all have this self-awareness, don't we? However, we'd all have to admit, rather sheepishly, 'Yeah, I've *sometimes* got it.'

Human beings have the capacity to be self-aware. It pops up when we are children, and strengthens until it reaches a usually painful pitch of intensity during adolescence. As we learn how to manage life more or less smoothly, we discover that we can daydream or go on automatic pilot without too many embarrassing disasters happening. So we slide in and out of that characteristically human, reflexive kind of consciousness.

In an emergency, we are suddenly right there, and we know we are. A car unexpectedly pulls out in front of us as we are driving, and we are completely alert as we take evasive action. Intense experiences also seem to induce self-awareness. A crucial race, an injury, romance, the bliss of wonderful music, embarrassment – again, we are right there and we know we are. But we also learn how to be *less* present, using drink or drugs for a more bleary experience of life, or distracting ourselves with escapist television. This seems to be evidence that a lot of life as it really is is too painful to be taken in fully.

Healthy self-awareness is called mindfulness in Buddhism, where it is a key virtue. The mirror analogy might be a bit misleading, because mindfulness doesn't mean watching yourself like a critical outside observer. Yes, you know what you're doing, and why you're doing it, and that it's *you* doing it. Yet your mindfulness is in the total situation, not just in an introspection that shuts out your sense experience and body sensations. Mindfulness has a flowing, vivid quality to it: you are immersed in life, experiencing its richness and acting upon it at the same time.

Are you mindful right now? This question highlights the mystery of mindfulness, I think. Assuming you were paying attention as you read the question, then as you wondered whether or not you were unmindful, the wondering itself was a mindful wondering. So why are we sometimes mindful and sometimes not? How can we be mindful more often, and does it matter?

It is worth considering all these issues because, for a Buddhist at least, yes, it does matter. We think we know what is happening, but if we are unmindful we miss so much. It's always better to know what's going on as fully as we can, because we are the creators of our own lives, and we have a big effect on the lives of others. Our lives and our influences can only be fruitful and rich if we are thoroughly present. This is partly because 'experience' is without meaning unless it is all actually experienced. And it is partly because, inevitably, we respond to our experiences and then very often we act, and, without intelligent guidance, responses can easily be peevish, and actions destructive. The guidance needs to come from ourselves at our best, at our most aware.

Cultivating mindfulness

So it's worth being mindful. It's worth consolidating the reflexive type of consciousness. You cultivate mindfulness by being attentive to your experience. Try this exercise:

Finding the mind 4[29]

First minute: What is your body up to now, and how are you holding your stomach and hands, what expression is on your face? And can you tell what mood you are in at present? You don't need to answer in words – simply notice. Notice, too, the thoughts passing through your mind.

Second minute: Now, with your eyes closed, pay attention to your breathing, the sensations of the air flowing in and out of your nose, and the moving muscles that expand and release the lungs. Fill your mind with the real experience of breathing, and repeatedly remember what you're doing. If you forget about the breath, which you probably will, patiently return your attention to it.

Third minute: Finally broaden your mindfulness, first back to your whole body. Open your eyes and get a sense of what is all around you, the sounds as well as colours and shapes. What *can't* you see – what comes to mind when you imagine the houses and streets nearby, people, clouds in the sky? And what is coming up – do you have a plan for when you put the book down?

Mindfulness can be a training: you can do mindfulness exercises. You appreciate and enjoy cultivating mindfulness where possible, so that the exercise is rewarding, but you try to stay mindful even when experience is uncomfortable; that's the time when you're most likely to learn about yourself and reality. You make an effort to pay attention all the time, but, because life is so complex, you will probably find you keep getting carried away from what is actually going on by thoughts about it, interpretations of it, and rehearsing what is coming next. Thoughts are fine if you are mindful of them, but the internal chatter easily deafens the still centre of awareness.

Special mindfulness meditation practices[30] generally work by asking you to focus your attention on one channel of experience, while you sit quietly and minimize the input through your senses. Your breathing gets the top prize among objects of attention for mindfulness meditation, as in the second minute of the three-minute mindfulness.

If you try the Mindfulness of Breathing, after a while, perhaps because the breath is so simple, quite subtle, and suffused with life, everything seems to quieten down. The breathing dominates your experience, and whatever else your mind is doing becomes clearer, easier to notice. You are in a mindful frame of mind, which is a state of well-established reflexive consciousness.

With mindfulness, you can take a second look in the mirror, the wheel of life. Outside the circle of the animal drives is a circle that is half black and half white. In the black half, naked people chained together tumble downwards; in the white half, colourfully dressed men and women move upwards as if on an escalator. Here we see there is a choice between what the Buddha called dark deeds and bright deeds. With mindfulness you can put energy into certain mental impulses and withdraw it from others; you can let some impulses express themselves in action, and restrain yourself from acting on others. This is Buddhist ethics, an ethics based in your knowledge of mental states, which offers the choice between skilful actions, the bright deeds, which genuinely benefit one's self and others, and unskilful, dark deeds, which cause harm and distress.

Degrees of awareness

Maybe poetry is better than philosophy or science for understanding the human mind, and in my opinion the Buddha was a fine poet:

> Far-ranging is the mind
> and it walks alone.
> It is not material.
> It sleeps
> in the cave of your heart.
> Keep it controlled
> and you're free from the bonds
> of death.[31]

There's one big surprise that I got from mindfulness practice, and I still haven't got used to it. That is how *changeable* and out of control my state of mind is. I'm far from getting over my insistence on a central authority-type Self, a solid 'I' watching everything and making all the decisions, which surely (I pretend) must be invariant, as the unstable world whirls around it. Yes, I know I can't find that central me anywhere, but my persistent imagining of it makes it quite a shock when it dawns on me that I've been so uneven in my mental states. For example, after a buoyant start today, later I was sunk in dullness, thoughts foggy for some time. Another time, after a day of irritability, I may suddenly notice it and have to acknowledge it's a mood, not an inexorable procession of very irritating people.

As the Buddha's poem says, our mind ranges far, over all sorts of terrain. Put simply, you can be more or less aware. In deep sleep, awareness is dimmed right down, and according to tradition there is just the glowing of the substrate consciousness, with no mental activity except for the stirring of seeds within it. Then there is dreaming sleep, then waking awareness. Meditative states form a whole hierarchy of increasing degrees of awareness, up to brilliantly illuminated states of absorption, where no thoughts interfere with watching the free play of the mind.[32]

It's interesting that Buddhist psychology focuses mainly on levels of consciousness from the normal human mind upwards, with a lot of advice on how to achieve less restricted mental states. Western psychology in contrast has been mainly interested in states of mind *more* restricted than the norm, especially pathological states and how they come about. Now the two psychologies are in dialogue, and this coincides with a greater interest in happiness and other healthy mental states among Western psychologists. Perhaps next will come a Western investigation of the process of awakening itself.

If heightened awareness is the important thing, what of the unconscious mind? For Sigmund Freud and his disciples, pathological states are generally connected with material repressed into 'the unconscious', popularly envisaged as a dark underground mental cellar in which ravenous beasts are chained up. In later Buddhism, the substrate is indeed 'unconscious', being seen as a source of impulses and tendencies that only emerge into awareness perhaps long after their seeds were planted.[33] Yet the image of seeds dormant in a substrate should not be taken literally; they are latent tendencies in a stream of mental events, not things in a place. That merry-go-round too – the animals at the hub of the wheel of life – is just a picture of deep tendencies, which have no life of their own.

All mental factors are seen as processes, as streams of events conditioning each other in complex ways. The metaphor of a dangerous cellar, a Pandora's box in which they lurk, doesn't really fit the Buddhist view. Processes occur that we are hardly aware of, 'below' the level of reflexive consciousness, but nothing is waiting for us 'in' an unconscious mind.

Mind evolving

Animals too have consciousnesses, in the sense that their mental processes do their best to work out what their sense experiences mean for them, and come up with appropriate behaviour. A fox sniffs the air, smells a dog, and swiftly turns tail. What animals almost certainly lack is reflexive consciousness, so they can't attend to their inner experience in the way they can attend to what comes to them through their senses, and they probably can't make deliberate, thought-out decisions on what to do next.

We are still members of the animal kingdom, and retain animal drives and instincts from our evolutionary past. We saw them in the first look in the mirror of the wheel of life. The third look shows us our animal nature once again, but it also shows us the range of other possibilities open to us as human beings. The third circle has five segments, literally called the 'goings' because they represent the realms of experience that one fares through on the journey of life. They are the types of mentality that we make our temporary homes in: the god realm, the human realm, the realm of torment, the realm of hunger, and the animal realm.[34]

If we take the 'goings' psychologically, we can probably recognize all five of them. When life is serene and rewarding we are in the god realm; when self-awareness brings perspective and empathy we are truly human; paranoia and despair belong to the realm of torment; inadequacy and feelings of never-satisfied longing keep us in the realm of hunger. The animal realm is when we avoid reflecting on our lives, and devote ourselves to the basic gratifications of food, comfort and procreation.

To reach the elevated vistas of self-awareness, animal consciousness evolved through millions of years, growing in its abilities with the enhancement of the senses and the nervous system.[35] The Buddha was not a biologist, and the world had to wait for Charles Darwin to discover evolution by natural selection. But it's surprising how intrinsically evolutionary Buddhism is. This is because it sees that an individual's mind can evolve into less and less restricted levels of consciousness, through processes whose hidden laws are consistent, and can be discovered. With one's mind evolving in one's own life, it is a welcome step to see life and minds evolving in the natural world too.

The Buddha explicitly rejected belief in a creator God. He said that all the phenomena we experience connect together in networks of connections: 'This being, that becomes. From the arising of this, that arises.'[36] For example, light shining on a tree and my eye being open and functioning are preconditions for me to notice the tree. Our experiences all arise from combinations of conditions, and the experiences are the conditions for our actions, and for more experiences. There are even Buddhist texts describing the conditions that account for the appearance of beings with self-awareness in the distant past. Buddhist stories of the origin of the human species are instructive myths rather than scientific accounts; yet they are evolutionary in approach, showing how human characteristics gradually emerge in an interplay with the environment.[37]

Consciousness in a chain

The role of consciousness in a sequence of conditional relations is the theme of the outermost circle of the wheel of life, revealed in another look in the mirror. It shows twelve links, where the last one joins the first to form a circle of eternal repetition, the wheel rolling relentlessly on. The five realms are a vision of the variety of general circumstances of life. The twelve links look more minutely at the chain of habitual mental events that keep us going round and round in circles.

The Buddha's great insight was to see the conditioned nature of all human experience, indeed of the whole of reality.[38] Nothing is separate, nothing is independent, nothing is stable. Every situation arose naturally from a preceding situation, and evolves naturally into something different. 'From the arising of this, that arises.' Our task is to discover the way situations link together, and use our discoveries to create a better life and a better world. To understand a situation, the key questions are: 'What conditions has this arisen in dependence upon? In dependence upon this, what new circumstances will arise?'

For example, if I spend more than an hour or two staring at a computer screen while the phone and visitors provide unpredictable interruptions, I become strained and bad-tempered. Talking from that bad temper, I pass my strain to others, and damage my relationships. Seeing the causal chain, I can interrupt it early on by taking a break, or even deciding to work differently.

We can find ourselves with a Janus-like awareness, its two faces looking in opposite directions, one gazing within and one without. For this reason, the Buddhist name for ordinary consciousness, *vijñāna*, can be analyzed to mean 'divided knowing',[39] an awareness that splits the world into me and not-me, and is thus divided from itself. The Buddha was convinced that he had discerned the factors that lead to this division in the mind, as well as seen how divided knowing leads to clinging, and gets us into all sorts of trouble. He summarized his insights in the twelve links:

The twelve links

1. In dependence upon ignorance, impulses arise.
2. In dependence upon the impulses, (the spark of) divided consciousness arises.
3. In dependence upon consciousness, the sentient body arises.
4. In dependence upon the sentient body, the six senses (including mind as a sense) arise.
5. In dependence upon the senses, contact arises.
6. In dependence upon contact, feeling arises.
7. In dependence upon feeling, craving arises.
8. In dependence upon craving, clinging arises.
9. In dependence upon clinging, renewed becoming arises.
10. In dependence upon becoming, birth arises.
11. In dependence upon birth arise ageing and death, sorrow, lamentation, pain, grief, and despair.
12. The twelfth link connects ageing, sorrow, and so on back to the beginning of the loop, ignorance.[40]

The links are sometimes explained as covering three lifetimes, with rebirth processes in between them. But it is also quite traditional to see them spinning through in brief instants of reactivity. There in our dim, ignorant substrate, the karmic seeds are active (1–2), and sooner or later they sprout as a spark of awareness (2). It is as if we 'come round' to find our dualistic selves (3) in a particular situation, eager to receive news of what is there (4), and sure enough something strikes through (5). Because of past associations, it has a particular tone to it, welcome or unwelcome (6), and if it is welcome, out of habit we want more of it (7), and we try to possess it (8). As a result, we slightly remould (9) our habits, even our personality, and emerge as a modified being (10). But the unskilful craving is a bad karma, and so the world that 'new' being experiences is filled with disappointment and distress (11). 'Such is the origin of this whole mass of suffering', concludes the Buddha.[41]

For example, tangled up in the confused remnants of my dreams (1–2), I wake up in the morning (2) already with mental stirrings like electrons whirling around a stiff body, their nucleus (3). My ears (4) take in the new day, a rushing sound (5), refreshing (6) even before I realize that it is the sound of heavy rain. I hope it carries on (7) because the garden so needs it, and I get fixated (8) on the idea that the drought is over, starting to plan what I'm doing (9) over the next few weeks, modifying my self-image (10) as my pictures of my future solidify. To the extent that all this is inflexible wishful thinking, it is setting me up for frustration (11), and my starting point of confusion (12) has reinforced itself. So far my predicament is not too bad, but it is by spinning through similar cycles over and over again that we create the mass of human suffering, including the pain and deprivation that we humans inflict upon each other, from bad neighbours to eco-crises and genocidal wars.

Finding the mind 5
Mirror exercise

Try this only if you feel comfortable with yourself, and have a gentle curiosity about your mind.

Find a mirror, preferably one that you can sit with, holding it in your hands and looking at your own face. Imagine you are seeing yourself as the Tibetan wheel of life. Spend about five minutes on each of the three stages.

First look: the three animal urges
Gaze softly at your own face, and see whether you can glimpse the aspect of yourself that needs, searches, and even hungers. That is the pigeon. See if you can catch sight of the aspect that is cautious and protective, pushing things away and attacking threats. That is symbolized by the snake. See if you can spot the aspect that is evasive, preferring less awareness to more awareness. That is the pig.

Second look: what realm are you in?
Sometimes we are a hungry ghost, sometimes an animal, sometimes an angel, sometimes a tormented victim, sometimes we are well balanced, well rounded – a human being. Can you see aspects of all these in your face? What is the predominant one at this time in your life?

Third look: the Buddha
Finally, take in your face, looking in a very soft and open way, seeing the depths, seeing the pains you have been through and the lessons you have learnt, seeing the richness of your background and your life, and just being aware of yourself as you are, with no judgement.

You don't have to revolve on this endless wheel: there is an alternative, and there are clues on the wheel of life, including a Buddha in each realm holding a symbol of self-liberation. Staying for now with the habitual, reactive chain, there is a little picture for each link. Consciousness is depicted as a monkey reaching for fruit in a tree. In the next chapter will see what the naughty monkey gets up to, and why it leads to such a melancholy 'mass of suffering'.

4

The Rills
of Selfishness

*All emotions are pure which gather you and lift you up; that
emotion is impure which seizes only one side of your being
and distorts you.*[42]

Rilke

Hoarding habits

The Buddha took care in choosing a relentlessly turning wheel
as an image for ordinary life. He felt there is something seriously
wrong with the way we live. We've learnt to get by in a certain
way; we've built up a cyclic, habitual approach in response to
experience, unrealistic and inflexible enough to account for the
deficiencies and anguish so prevalent in human life. The Buddha
insisted that the primary issue is not wickedness, but ignorance.
The monkey of the mind knows what it likes, and it is not prepared
to come down from its little tree and look for that ancient road to
the city of awakening.

Remember that the mind is divided in the sense that it splits
into two the experiences that flow through it: some coming from

within, some coming from an outer world. It assumes that 'inner' experience must come from a Self, which it fervently believes in, and frantically tries to protect. So it's made a mistake, it views things unrealistically in all sorts of ways, and because we live from this mistake, we cause harm to ourselves and others, not originally from wickedness, but from habitual ignorance. In this chapter I want to look at the unskilful habits and behaviours that follow from our primordial mistake.

Think of your room or your house, preferably somewhere where you have lived for several years. You're probably surrounded by your habits there, habits that have become solidified into things. Your favourite books, posters, or CDs. Maybe some photos of people, maybe knick-knacks on the mantelpiece; how you dress, your daily programme. The alarm clock and the radio, the diary and bits of paper – they all keep the secret of how you spend your days. And frozen habits pile up: books to read one day, dusty gifts, cupboards full of saucepans. Yes, they all hold the comforts of home, but do they also feel constraining? That place is full of the messages of habits. Granted some of them are good habits, but many are not so good.

My father's house was like that. My father was unusually rich in fine qualities. I loved him dearly, and in his house you could see his many interests – in religion, science, electronics and machinery, human nature, Egyptian deities. But his house also displayed his weaknesses. I had the task of sorting out his possessions after he died. It took about a year, because the place was crammed with things, papers and books in heaps, like a badly organized archaeological dig.

The things reminded me of his remarkable qualities. They also made me feel sombre, because they often said to me: 'Here was Dad, doodling with his life by collecting things, hoarding notions, polishing up outdated habits.' And then he died, in the middle of it all, in a sense a prisoner not just of his piles of possessions, but of the loops of his self-confirming ideas, loops like nooses of rope, like iron shackles that kept him chained in habit.

In many ways I feel I am not so different from my father. Then I think of the years ahead. When I am caught by 'the Lord of Death's rough-coated hounds', will I still be tangled up in my habits? Have I got anything really new to do, or at least to experience?

One of Lawrence Durrell's characters says this:

> It's a terrible thing to feel that one has come to the end of one's life experience – that there is nothing fundamentally new to look forward to: one must expect more and more combinations of the same sort of thing – the thing which has proven one a sort of failure. So then you start on the declining path, living a sort of posthumous life, your blood cool, your pulse steady ... And yet it is just the fruitful point at which some big new understanding might jump out on you from behind the bushes and devour you like a lion.[43]

Insecurity

It seems rather depressing, this idea of being trapped in mouldering habits, though getting downhearted by the unsatisfactoriness of life is itself just a rather deadening habit. But something, the lion of a new understanding, wants to break through the limitations of habit. To make the breakthrough, I have to see what's going on, I have to understand why I hold on to my habitual ways of responding.

George Eliot says of one of her villains: 'The little rills of selfishness had united and made a channel so that they could never again meet with the same resistance.'[44] Self-orientation seems to be the characteristic of all the limiting, restricting kinds of habits. It is not just that I happen to do things in a particular way because I'm used to it. Deep down, behind my habits, there is a sense that I have to protect myself, there is an unnecessary sense of insecurity.

Imagine those times when we don't *have* to be habitual. We can size up the whole situation, see it in the light of what we're trying to achieve, and then act wholeheartedly, spontaneously, appropriately. But often I'm incapable of doing that, and I think the main reason is this insecurity. The old habitual ways are reassuring. They are me, they define for me who I am. For example, sometimes when I'm walking in the countryside, instead of being fully there, I fill my mind with anxious and busy little thoughts. It seems as if I am trying to give a sort of solidity and predictability to my experience.

The most obvious self-protective habits are called in Buddhism the 'mine-making' process, and they come from a straightforward craving for externals, like food, possessions, or a lover. More subtle are what are called the 'I-making' habits: views around what we identify with. Most subtle of all are the 'I am' habits, known as conceit. It is said that you can recognize whether somebody is awakened by evaluating these three: mine-making, I-making, and the 'I am' conceit.[45] Holding to 'I am' is the last vestige of operating from a split awareness. Before we can hope to dissolve such a subtle habit, we need to tackle cravings and I-making.

Mine-making and I-making

Because our sense of self is rather precarious, beleaguered even, we tend habitually either to reach out to or push away whatever we encounter, usually in ways that are quite subtle and hard to notice. Reaching out for things is the mine-making process, our tendency to 'selfish attachment or self-interest'.[46] The things may be actual possessions, but can also relate to one's own body and appearance. So mine-making is a habitual grasping for, for example:

- my dwelling;
- my garden;
- my home decor;
- my holiday destination;
- my choice of clothing;
- my hairstyle;
- my gender;
- my sexual preferences;
- my facial expressions;
- my voice ... and many more.

I can even *identify* myself in terms of where I live, what I look like, and so on. Often, though, my identity is bound up with internals, not external things. A fixed identity is the story we tell ourselves, and others, of who we are, of what defines us. The identity story can be a sort of catalogue of preferences – *these* experiences I find pleasant and go for, *these* experiences I find unpleasant and avoid; and 'I' am summed up by that catalogue. I tend to give everything in my life a little static electric charge, so it seems to carry an intrinsic attraction or repulsion.

Objectively, however, preferences are pretty arbitrary. They are just habits, and none are *actually* valid or invalid (though some basic preferences are deeply instinctive, for good survival reasons). My preferences are reinforced by what I tell people, and by a sort of internal monologue. For example, I arrive at the breakfast table on holiday, and easily fall into a little listing: 'Oh good, there's honey, I like honey, but I'm not keen on all the flowery napkins and tablecloths; I can smell something good coming from the kitchen, I like China tea...' And so it goes on. A stranger walks into the dining room, and immediately there are little half-conscious responses of attraction, interest, or dismissal, perhaps reinforced by little mental comments.

Likes and dislikes are conditioned things. They are the legacy of our past, being the second of the five clusters, our habitual felt responses. A few of them go back into our evolutionary past, but most of them have been built up through experiences in childhood and since. Why the hell do I like tea and not coffee, when my friend with almost identical taste buds is the other way round? It's quite instructive to try pretending that you like something that usually you'd vigorously avoid.

I was once on a long Buddhist retreat where the participants decided to wear monastic-style robes, to make it all feel more authentic in various ways. My goodness, I hated the robes! I was muttering to myself about how stupid they looked, how impractical and uncomfortable they were, and I wanted to wear *my* clothes. But after a while, I realized that it was simply dislike – it wasn't really to do with whether they were appropriate or not. I noticed a half-deliberate fog that descended over my mind when I tried to distinguish between what really matters and what was just a personal preference. And to my shame, I realized how strongly I was ruled by my likes and dislikes, how restricted by the process of 'I-making'. After that realization, I never came to like the stupid things, but I did wear them with relative equanimity!

A.A. Milne's fictional teddy bear follows his own footsteps in the snow round and round a spinney of trees, thinking he is tracking a wild woozle.[47] Similarly, our preferences are the fossil footprints of old habits, followed blindly round and round in circles. They are not deliberate – they just happen. I can't change the past, so these preferences are bound to arise whenever I'm passive to experience. But I can change the *future*. The unreflective consequence of getting something I like is craving more of it, and aversion if I don't like it. So likes and dislikes lead to craving, then clinging, and so making a new 'I', in the process described on the outer circle of the wheel of life.

How to change the mind's future when it is so habit-bound? The Buddhist method is always to notice. You notice the habits. You notice the clinging and even the craving that precedes it. Best of all, you spot what is going on at the earliest possible point – you notice the feeling of like or dislike, and stay with it without sliding through into craving, clinging, and the rest. Mindfulness practice means staying with the experience, and letting it be as it is without turning it into a great drama of mine-making or I-making.

A new criterion for action

However, you won't always notice every event in bare experience. Therefore, the first stage of a Buddhist life is to move the seat of government from the likes-and-dislikes polarity to that of skilful and unskilful, the bright and dark deeds of the wheel of life, the criteria of Buddhist ethics. You restrain the craving, the clinging, and the other self-protective responses, and you see whether you can stop yourself turning those mental responses into harmful words and deeds.

Being governed by likes and dislikes means you will sometimes be unskilful, since all craving comes from the wish to perpetuate pleasant experiences, and all aversion from a wish to escape unpleasant ones. It makes so much sense, if we find something gratifying, to hang on to it (though simply enjoying what we like is not itself unskilful). But what happens is that we fix something as a provider of pleasure, grasping it to make it 'mine', while all the time the pleasure was not the gift of the something itself. The something had a significance for us, triggered certain associations, and so our encounter with it brought us pleasure. So, for example, I have met a certain person, and I love her company, so I want her to be *mine*. But the more I expect her to play a role in the life-drama in which I star, being a certain person just for me, the more quickly she will assert her own different needs, and we will fall out, probably both feeling betrayed. Even inanimate possessions fail us in the same way. Mine-making is a clinging; clinging is an unskilful state leading to frustration sooner or later. Aversion is the mirror image of this.

The consequence of craving and aversion is that things go wrong, and life becomes unsatisfactory because the world does not match your wants. This is how unskilfulness is defined in Buddhism: it comes from craving and aversion, and it leads to frustration and misery.[48] By definition, unskilful actions harm yourself and others. Skilful actions in contrast come from open and loving states, and lead to benefit and happiness.

Leaving behind likes and dislikes as your motivator will sound disconcerting to some. Yet it does not mean a swap to *not* doing what you want to do and *doing* what you dislike. Skilful/unskilful are categories of a different nature from like/dislike. You are choosing on the basis of skilfulness instead of giving in to the mine-making habit, and a skilful choice can be tough, but it is often delightful. It can be very skilful to do what you like, and pleasant experiences are often the consequences of previous skilfulness. Ruling your life by always choosing what you like, hedonism, leads to disappointment and selfishness. But ruling your life by what you *don't* like is religious asceticism, a practice the Buddha tried before his awakening, and emphatically found did not help. He reflected: 'Why am I afraid of such pleasure?' Then he explored the delights to be found in a clarified human mind – a skilful mind.[49]

In my experience happiness does *not* come from passively doing the washing-up even though I don't feel like it. Happiness accompanies being so fired up to make a real difference in the world that washing-up (or not) is no longer the issue at all. If doing the washing-up makes a helpful difference, then just do it, and it may well be quite fun after all.

Unskilful impulses

The dynamo of the wheel of life is the trio of animals at the centre, representing craving, aversion, and ignorance. Ignorance is the primary one, and according to Buddhism it is basically the mistaken belief that within us is a vulnerable and hungry Self. We are rather like a tiny bird desperately finding food for an enormous cuckoo chick that is never satisfied – if only we knew that that monster has nothing to do with us.

But we are so busy feeding the Self that there always seems to be a shortage, always the fear of not meeting its needs. So depending on the particular challenges life throws at us, a great crowd of other unskilful impulses arise. Here are a few of them:

Some unskilful mental states from the Buddhist tradition[50]

- Craving
- Vindictive anger
- Arrogance
- Wilful unawareness
- Indecisiveness
- Opinionated views
- Indignation
- Resentment
- Slyness-concealment
- Defensiveness
- Envy
- Acquisitiveness
- Pretence

- Dishonesty
- Self-inflation
- Cruelty
- Lack of self-respect
- Lack of respect for the wise
- Mental stagnation
- Ebullience
- Lack of confidence in the positive
- Laziness
- Heedlessness
- Unmindfulness
- Purposelessness
- Distraction

Skilful effort

Completely overcoming primordial ignorance, the mistakes that lead to unskilful impulses and actions, is the task of a lifetime. But Buddhism recommends making a start right away by noticing the harmful things that we do, restraining ourselves from them, and replacing them with actions that make a positive difference to ourselves and others. That is, shifting the reasons for our actions to a basis of skilful and unskilful. We can learn to recognize what is skilful and what is unskilful. There are two complementary ways of learning this: seeing the ethical value of the states of mind we are in, and recognizing the results of actions. Gradually, with the help of labels such as those listed above, we sense that *these* states are restricted and self-serving, *those* are expansive. We see the restrictive ones cause trouble to ourselves and others, while the expansive ones make things work out better. Thus we can change the way we live. Living more ethically tends to undermine self-centred states of mind. Even ignorance itself is challenged by how we live.

Think of the immense relief of living without insecurity, because we are no longer stuck in protecting an illusory Self. The Buddha says we are like a dog whose lead is looped around a post so it can only run round and round in circles: the post is a fixed view of what one thinks of as one's Self.[51]

So, to some extent, we are composed of habit, and on top of that we regard ourselves in habit-bound ways. Accumulating tokens of security, we are caught up in mine-making. Reciting our preferences and identifying ourselves as 'like this', we make the I, too. Not to identify with anything sounds rather precarious. However, in the same way that strong self-awareness is possible without attachment to a Self, a strong, identifiable personality is possible without strongly identifying. And if we could completely drop habitual self-view, we would join, says the Buddhist tradition, the main current to awakening. Ceasing to insist on our own specialness, we'd also have a natural sense of solidarity with others – the lasso of compassion.

5

The Lasso
of Compassion

the life
at which I aim
is a circumference
continually expanding
through sympathy and
understanding
rather than an exclusive centre
of pure self-feeling
the whole I seek
is centre plus circumference
and now the struggle at the centre is over
the circumference
beckons from everywhere.[52]

Kenneth White

Holding a gem

The emblem of Buddhism is the meditating Buddha. Everywhere you go in Buddhist countries, in Buddhist temples, in Buddhist homes, you will see pictures and statues of the Buddha serenely sitting in meditation, gently smiling through the deep contentment of awakening. But Buddhist art isn't confined to depictions of the Buddha. In most Buddhist countries you will also find images of youthful princes and princesses, flamboyantly dressed, seated on lotus blossoms. These are the Bodhisattvas – mythical beings displaying the exuberance of the cavalcade to awakening. The best known is the Bodhisattva of compassion, whom we met in female form in chapter 1 advising the monk on his meditation. On the wheel of life he appears in male form in each of the five realms, displaying an object that symbolizes the way out. The Tibetan form in the illustration has his hands clasped at his breast in the Indian gesture of greeting. In some versions you will see a glow between his fingers, perhaps rays of light darting out. His hands are cradling a glinting gem, and that gem represents his mind, a transformed mind crucial in the schools of Buddhism that emphasize compassionate activity. It is known as the Bodhi mind.

'Bodhi' is the word for 'awakening', here awakening with a strong altruistic emphasis. It is said to be a state of being in which all traces of defensive separateness from others have vanished, like the darkness that flees when a lamp is brought into a room at night.[53]

Like a lamp, the mind shines naturally with the radiance of awareness. The Buddha said: 'The mind is luminous, [when it] is cleansed of the defilements that come from without.'[54] Our awareness in itself is simply open to the way things actually are, but we have deep habits of unnecessarily protecting a fictitious Self. These overlay our simple awareness with encrustations that hide and distort the way things are. But it doesn't have to be like that: our mind can be 'cleansed'.

The Bodhi mind is thus a completely cleansed mind, or at least a mind that is determined to be cleansed, absolutely set upon awakening. You could see the cradling hands of the Bodhisattva

Figure 5

of compassion as gradually opening to reveal the full glory of the gem of Bodhi mind. In fact, the mantra of this Bodhisattva, the sacred phrase recited repeatedly when you meditate on him, is sometimes said to refer to a gem hidden in an opening lotus bud.[55] We are like tightly closed water-lily buds, ready to open organically, in our own time, if the sun is warm enough, eventually to reveal this beautiful jewel nestling in the calyx.

Yes, a flowery simile. But it refers back to an image used by the Buddha to represent human potential – he saw humanity as like a pond full of lotuses, with the plants and flowers in all stages of development, everyone having the potential to blossom fully.[56]

What is it that obscures the Bodhi mind? There are said to be two veils, one emotional and one cognitive. The first is the veil of self-centred unskilful drives such as craving, hatred, fear, envy, and so on. The second is the veil of views, of misconceptions about the way things are, mainly springing from attachment to a Self. Really, the veils are us limiting our awareness, in order to be self-protective and self-interested. So the Bodhi mind is a mental stance that goes beyond self-interest, the altruistic mind of a Bodhisattva.

Because human awareness is like this naturally, we already have a hint of its radiance; it is so brilliant that light sometimes briefly flashes through. But Bodhi mind is said properly to arise when there is a definite chink in the encrustations that surround it, so that there is *always* some light shining through. Dualistic mind has to some extent changed into an open mind.[57]

Breaking down the barriers

That's the image – now what about the practicalities? If we could get Bodhi mind to arise, we wouldn't be fully awakened yet, but we'd have a clear *sense* of awakening. We'd have opened a communication channel with reality, a channel unobscured by the two veils. So you could say the grand preliminary project of Buddhism is to get your Bodhi mind to arise.

In chapter 2, I described the fenced-in patch of garden in the substrate, the patch that our self-interested mind so tenaciously defends. Bodhi mind wouldn't do that. Would it be possible to break down the fence? The fence represents our artificial boundaries, and the most crucial border that we guard is the one designed to keep out other people. Now, there is a meditation practice that culminates in what is called 'breaking down the barriers' with other people.[58] It does so by progressively cultivating a very strong friendly response to all the people in our world.

The meditation starts with self-friendliness, softening your defensiveness by evoking a warm and open mood, one of confidence in your emotional strength, so you feel less fixated on protective barriers. You edge out the usual anxious inner voice with one that says, 'It's fine to want happiness and a good life; I already know what that's like, go for it! And that's what everyone else wants too.' So you first recall a close friend, and notice the natural well-wishing, how relatively easy it is to go out to them with a softer edge. Now you see whether you can maintain that soft welcoming and friendly response if you think of a neutral person and even somebody who is difficult, whom you would normally avoid. Then you start testing those barriers, by holding all four people including yourself in your heart simultaneously, without excluding any from the friendly welcoming atmosphere.

In the last stage of the meditation, you allow the loving awareness that you have built up to expand and radiate outwards, imagining more and more people and other living beings, and consciously noticing any boundaries that still remain, letting the goodwill melt them away.

Finding the mind 6
The friendliness meditation[59]
Sit quietly, and spend between two and five minutes on each of these stages:

- Bring to mind your healthy wish for your own welfare and happiness, and hold it in your heart.
- Bring to mind a close friend, and let your wish go out to them.

- Bring to mind a neutral person, including them as well.
- Bring to mind someone you find difficult, yet keep the intense friendliness alive.
- Include all four of you in an atmosphere of friendliness.
- Expand and radiate the friendliness to everybody.

Others matter as much as I do

The eighth-century Buddhist philosopher-poet Śāntideva presents a long argument for a loving awareness of others, an awareness that gives them the same priority as oneself. Here are some of the points he makes:

> One should cultivate the [Bodhi mind like this].
>
> One should first earnestly meditate on the equality of oneself and others in this way: 'All equally experience suffering and happiness, and I must protect them as I do myself.'
>
> Just as the body, which has many parts owing to its division into arms and so forth, should be protected as a whole, so should this entire world, which is differentiated and yet has the nature of the same suffering and happiness.
>
> Although my suffering does not cause pain in other bodies, nevertheless that suffering is mine and is difficult to bear because of my attachment to myself.
>
> Likewise, although I myself do not feel the suffering of another person, that suffering belongs to

that person and is difficult [for him] to bear because of his attachment to himself.

I should eliminate the suffering of others because it is suffering, just like my own suffering. I should take care of others because they are sentient beings, just as I am a sentient being.

When happiness is equally dear to others and myself, then what is so special about me that I strive after happiness for myself alone?

When fear and suffering are equally abhorrent to others and myself, then what is so special about me that I protect myself but not others?[60]

So the idea is of a transformation of the mind, in which you let go of self-preoccupation, and replace it not with cold indifference but with an intense concern for the well-being of everybody, including yourself. This is a very ambitious endeavour. You attempt it by becoming more sensitive to the boundaries that form around self-interest, finding ways of dissolving those boundaries.[61]

The paradox of compassion

You might say: 'If there is no abiding core of selfhood in anybody, why care about them, why bother about their suffering?' Śāntideva hints at a response in the passage quoted above, and so does the friendliness meditation. If seeing through Self led one not to be bothered at all about suffering, then one would abandon one's *own* welfare and interests straight away, as well as other people's. But actually one *does* have a deep concern for one's own happiness and well-being, and this does not have to be a narrow, fearful, self-protective concern. It is the start of the genuine benevolence that can expand to include everybody else.

In a way, someone with the Bodhi mind is a living paradox. He or she is desperate to promote the happiness and relieve the suffering of everybody he or she encounters. Yet the ancient illusion of beings substantially existing has been seen through. Somehow both truths, though apparently contradictory, are held at once. The first is compassion, the second is wisdom – the two faces of awakening.

The Buddha describes this dual perspective in the *Diamond Sūtra*:

> Someone who has set out in the vehicle of a
> bodhisattva should produce a thought in this manner:
> 'as many beings as there are in the universe of beings ...
> all these must I lead to Nirvāṇa ... And yet ... no being
> at all has been led to Nirvāṇa.' And why? ... He is not
> to be called a Bodhi-being [Bodhisattva] in whom the
> notion of a self or of a being should take place, or the
> notion of a living soul or of a person.[62]

The problem is holding on to unhelpful notions about people, pretending to know exactly who they are and what they need, impeding genuine helpfulness.

For this reason, there is said to be a scale of compassion. Compassion is sympathy for others, especially when you are aware of their suffering. At first it is a sympathy still caught in the delusion of an ultimate separation between self and other. When you see profoundly that suffering arises from a mistaken self-belief, you have a deeper compassion, informed by a more realistic attitude, some glimpse of the ultimate truth. Even here you are still conceptualizing other people, focusing on them as if truly existent. Fully awakened compassion, the highest kind, is said to 'overwhelm' any idea of a separate self.[63] If you have realized that the boundary between you and another person is fabricated by your self-protective notions, then any motivation for well-being seeks well-being for all.

The jewel net

The human mind is a jewel. It is precious, it is beautiful, it refracts the world's sunlight into flickering rainbows, and it seems to sparkle with its own inner fire. Does yours feel like that? It's quite a strain living this human life, living under the pressure of expectations, especially our own. So our mind can feel boxed in, the jewel can feel clutched and squeezed in dirty hands. With a bit of space and patience, we can loosen the grip and notice dazzling rays flashing between our fingers. Oh the relief of letting go!

To experience something as being precious and beautiful is to love it. We can love, even adore, the magical awareness that is our companion all the time, or better that simply is *us*. When awareness is allowed to shine, when the busy thinking of self-concern is in abeyance, our world too shines, and beauty and significance become manifest even in a rusting railway bridge, in a pigeon eyeing a discarded hamburger. 'To the dull mind, all nature is leaden', says Emerson. 'To the illuminated mind the whole world burns and sparkles with light.'[64]

But let's not get completely caught up in our own mind, or in railway bridges and hamburgers. Because, wonder of wonders, we keep bumping into other people. And each one of them, without exception, holds a jewel of awareness as precious and beautiful as our jewel. When we meet somebody else it's so easy to shrink back into a tight self-concern, and once again pouch that shining gem inside a hard fist. Others tend to seem vaguely threatening, slightly repugnant, uninteresting, or rather alluring – all responses that bracket them in terms of our needs and expectations. Is it possible to see them instead as being their own special jewels of bright awareness, all of our beams criss-crossing like a laser display?

It's like the net of the Indian thunder-god, Indra. In Hindu tradition, one of his weapons is a net as big as the sky to trap his enemies, but in Chinese Buddhism this becomes a delicate lacework that spans the cosmos, a jewel at every node, so that:

> Hundreds of thousands of jewels are reflected in
> every individual jewel, and each jewel is reflected in
> hundreds of thousands of jewels. Centre jewel and
> surrounding jewels reflect back and forth, multiplying
> and remultiplying the images endlessly.[65]

The net image indicates how all people, indeed all things, are discrete and do not obstruct each other's individuality, but yet are not separate, so that each reflects all the others.

So our mind can unveil itself as the jewel-like Bodhi mind if we can cleanse it of its surface defilements of self-clinging and self-view. Opening to others with friendliness and compassion will help this to happen. Whenever you encounter an edge to yourself, find out how to step over it. Then step over it, and see what happens.

Maybe that's enough, but it may be that we have to do some deep delvings into the jewel mine of our consciousness to find Bodhi mind and bring it to the surface. As well as compassion, we need wisdom, understanding the structure of our mind and working to perfect it.

6

I Am a Miner
for a Heart of Gold

*To study the Buddha way is to study the self. To study the
self is to forget the self. To forget the self is to be actualized
by myriad things. When actualized by myriad things, your
body and mind, as well as the bodies and minds of others,
drop away. No trace of realization remains, and this no-trace
continues endlessly.*[66]

Dōgen

Helpful habits

Buddhism is concerned with human experience. It says that,
by and large, human experience is very unsatisfactory. We are
plagued by all sorts of disappointment, loss, and grief. Is this
necessary? No – it happens because of mistaken perception,
because of not seeing things as they are.

Repeatedly, our dawning awareness is dismayed by the sheer
scale and richness of the reality presented to it. So it clutches
at what is nearest to hand – it commandeers a local patch of
experience as its home, calling it 'I', and gathering around it a

reassuring collection of 'mine'. Then it lives an impoverished life, imagining rivals and petty worries that threaten its security.

If we want really to inhabit the vastness and richness of our world, we have somehow to liberate ourselves from this mistake. How to do it? We need methods for freeing ourselves from the bonds of habit, from the unskilful habits we saw in chapter 4. The Buddha once said that you can tell whether something is genuinely Buddhism or not according to whether it has the taste of freedom.[67] Many approaches have that liberating taste. Where can we start? Habitual, defended mind is the root, but it is easier to start with its effects in the way we live.

It would be lovely just to drop every habitual response, and be spontaneous, so that one was wonderful, and loved by all, like some Robin Hood. There are two problems, though. One is that, if I act spontaneously when I'm in unskilful states of mind, states like neediness or insecurity, then I'll just cause a lot of grief. The other is that I am *habitually* habitual – I can't just switch on the spontaneity at will.

But it's not so bad, because habits can be progressive; in other words, we can take up ethical habits, 'good' habits if you like, or better, *skilful* habits. At first, it feels a bit awkward to restrain a tendency to snarl at people, say. Maybe I can't even *see* any ethical improvements I can make. But I just take on the Buddhist ethical precepts of not harming living beings and so on.[68] Then I get a few friends to keep me to my resolutions, and eventually vegetarianism and honesty (say) are almost second nature – skilful habits.

This practice of being ethical starts off with a certain degree of clarity about what matters in life. Really being prepared to think things through, see what the alternatives are, decide on my priorities, and then adjust the way I live.

Living better is just a start. Somehow the barriers we have erected within our mind still need to be broken down. In the last chapter we saw how the crucial barriers are those that divide us from others, and there are ways of vaulting over them, and delighting in a solidarity with all that lives. The Buddha calls this process 'the liberation of mind through universal friendliness'. Twinned with this path is a 'liberation through wisdom', in which our mistakes are confronted directly in the most closely guarded recesses of our self-cherishing.[69] In later Buddhism, the two types of liberation are erected as inseparable twin pillars of the arch of awakening – compassion and wisdom. Let's look at liberation through wisdom.

The architecture of the mind

I started the last chapter by describing the central emblem of Buddhism, the seated figure of the awakened Buddha. Buddhism also has a fundamental architectural form, the stūpa, which evolved into the pagoda in East Asia.

The stūpa is not a building that you go into, but one that you walk round and round in moving meditation, keeping the stūpa on your right as a reminder of the enlightened mind. Stūpas originate before Buddhism, in the royal burial mounds of ancient India. When the earth goddess was all-powerful, soil was heaped over the ruler's ashes, and then encased in unbaked bricks, to form what was called a 'womb mound' or 'egg mound'. At the same time there was an opposing kind of religion around, based on fire and sky gods, where the ceremonies were sacrifices held on an altar under the village tree.

The first Buddhist stūpas were constructed to house the ashes of the Buddha himself and his awakened disciples, and they seem to have united the earth and sky spiritualities. Generally, the mound became a solid plastered dome, built on a platform, with a fire altar on the top and a shaft leading down into the centre of the mound. After cremation the ashes fell into the centre,

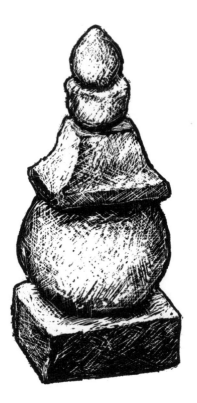

Figure 6

and an elegant parasol was erected on the very top, the Indian symbol of sovereignty. Already, the Buddhist stūpa symbolizes psychological integration, the earthy parts of us uniting with the fire or sky parts of us.

Every Buddhist country has its characteristic forms of the stūpa. Over time, the monuments took on more and more symbolic significance, which was eventually simplified into a composition of pure form, representing the elements that make up the universe, which are reflected in the structure of the human mind. The purest version of this five-element stūpa to be found in actual physical structures fills the Buddhist graveyards of Japan.[70]

Table 1 Elements of the stūpa

Original component	New shape	Element symbolized
Basal platform	Yellow cube	Earth – solidity and support
Mound	White sphere	Water – fluidity and cohesion
Fire altar	Red cone	Fire – heat and chemical energy
Royal parasol	Green dish shape	Air – motion and expansion
Surmounting gem (possibly)	Scintillating jewel drop	Radiant space

You can see the gradual liberation of the mind as the stage-by-stage construction of the stūpa. We start with the strong base of earth. This is whatever is solid, supportive, and unmoving in our experience, resisting with rigidity. The elements are not literal components of matter, like the elements of the periodic table in the West. They represent ways in which our apparently external experience *resists* us.[71]

Each of the elements is called a 'great conjuror', in the sense that we can never know what is there independently of our experience – we can only know what it seems like, from the way it resists our probing. So an experience of something hard and unyielding is of the great conjuror we call the earth element. If our experience is *only* earth element, we are like somebody trussed up in a prison, unable to move at all.

The beginning of liberation is symbolized by the water element; water sloshes back and forth in a bowl, and similarly we can find ourselves not completely immobilized, but able to oscillate back and forth between opposites. Pain and pleasure, obscurity and popularity, success and failure, manic energy and depressed lethargy, or whatever.

Fire whooshes up in an alarming way, and the fire element brings a second, vertical dimension into our experience, in the sense that blissful and exalted states of consciousness become accessible. However, you may rise up like a firework, getting all excited and idealistic, but losing touch with the earth, and perhaps ending in a shower of sparks.

Air represents expansion, moving outwards in all directions. It symbolizes freedom and flexibility. But if you get intoxicated by the thrill of expansion and lose sight of the other elements, you get spread out over too many things. You are so universal and at one with everything that you've become completely undifferentiated, and you don't really care what happens. Everything is fine. This might sound good, but I think it's a very dangerous state to be in.

The brilliant sparkling drop at the very top of the stūpa seems an odd image for space. But in this context we are not talking about the black silent vastness between the planets, but the radiant 'inner' space in which all objects of awareness manifest. As a symbol, the space drop represents liberated mind in which all the other elements are playing their positive and supportive role.

So the stūpa illustrates a spiritual process of integrating and developing your mind. You must start with the firm and solid earth; you must bring in the receptive container of the water element, taking the shape of whatever it occupies. You need to learn to rise up like a flame as well, experiencing the heights and the depths, finding inspiration perhaps in art and poetry, and finding bliss in deep spiritual experiences. Then you need to have the expansiveness of air, moving outwards, encountering the new, filling the space around you. Then you need the single jewel drop of being completely awake in every situation.

The inner and outer elements

The construction of a spiritual stūpa is the work of a lifetime. But the whole sequence can be recapitulated within a meditation session, using the structured contemplation of the elements. In this traditional form of the meditation, there are six elements rather than five, space and the awareness or consciousness that illuminates it being distinguished from each other.

The meditation itself requires proper personal instruction. But I'd like to take you through the reflection procedure. It is an attempt to purify our awareness. In a quiet meditative frame of mind, we are challenging the ego-based attitudes that keep the mind restricted as well as destructive.

We are trying to become aware of the six elements in our experience, as ways in which our perception of the world meets with various forms of resistance. Then we are reflecting on their nature, and recognizing that they can't be owned (mine-making) and that they can't house a fixed self (I-making). As a result, we can let go both of attachment to them and of identification with them, ultimately dropping body and mind altogether, as in the Zen quotation from Dōgen that opened this chapter.

Finding the mind 7
The elements

We can notice, deeply, the earth element, everything solid in the world around us, and also directly feel it in our body. Notice how the solidity in our body is basically the same as whatever is solid outside our body, so it would be foolish to identify any separate and autonomous self in the solid parts of us, or as being composed of the solid parts. In fact, the earth in us is derived from solid food that we've eaten, showing that it is dependent on external things as well as being indistinguishable from them. What is more, all the molecules of our body are just temporary guests – after a while we give back everything solid in our body to the outside world as if it was only borrowed. We do this all the time through excretion and so on; and when we die, the whole lot will be returned to the earth. The sameness, dependence, and impermanence of the earth element in our body show that there can be no isolated, independent, or permanent self associated with the earth element. 'It is not me, it is not mine, it is not the self.'[72]

The same reflections are relevant to the water, fire, and air elements. We reflect on all that is liquid in our body, all the warmth and chemical energy, and all the air or vitality that we can notice in our body. All of them can't be 'me or mine' in any ultimate sense, because they are engaged in a constant exchange, largely outside our control, with the same elements in the external world. So, with relief, we can let go of attachment to each element in turn, resting in a sense of freedom from it.

Even space is like that – the room our body takes up, the locations that we identify with, we may be very fond of them, protective of them, but we can't hold on to them.

The consciousness element

What about consciousness, the sixth element? The other five elements sum up our body – there is nothing else but them in our physical make-up. Consciousness is, or seems, whatever is aware of and through our body; it is because consciousness is somehow caught up with the other internal elements that we tend to think of them as me or mine, so it is rather different. You can reflect like this: '*Here* is a consciousness that is limited by being tied to other things. It is bound up with the other elements forming the body, with sense experience, and with rational, discriminative thought. *Here* is a ceaseless flow of mental events.'

Each moment of consciousness is, according to traditional

Buddhism, a distinct event. It is momentary, flashing into being at the moment of contact with an object. The next moment another instant of consciousness comes into being, with an object that itself is now something fresh, slightly different from before. Thus we have a stream of awareness of shifting objects. Each momentary consciousness arises in dependence upon contact with the object, and upon the remnants of consciousnesses before it, and it moves as the object does. This is not intended as a theory, but as a straightforward attempt to describe what we actually experience. Something so transitory, surely, cannot be me or mine, cannot be myself.

It all takes place in a context of a great variety of possible states of mind, all of them potentially accessible to us. The human mind can be less restricted. At the moment, our mind is restricted because it is bound up with the body, the senses, and thinking. We can disentangle from whatever pops up in our awareness, letting it flow through, not identifying with any of it. Trying to watch what is there without the anxious sense that it's all crucial to 'myself'. Letting go into a clear, spacious, non-centred illumination, which is awareness itself.

By watching the contents of the mind and letting them go, we are accepting our habitual duality, and in a sense seeing our consciousness 'objectively'. More subtly, we can reflect that awareness is there, but it can't be *observed*, by definition, as a subject.

An ancient sūtra describes it like this:

> Searching for mind all around, he does not see it
> within or without. He does not see it in the [clusters],
> or in the elements or in the sense-fields. Unable to see
> consciousness, he seeks to find the trend of his mind,
> and asks himself: 'Whence is the genesis of mind?' And
> it occurs to him that 'where there is an object, there

mind arises.' Is then mind one thing, and the object another? No, what is the object, just that is the mind. If the object were one thing, and the mind another, then there would be a double state of mind. So the object itself is just mind.

Can then mind review mind? No, mind cannot review mind. As the blade of a sword cannot cut itself, so a mind cannot see itself. Moreover, vexed and pressed hard on all sides, mind proceeds, without any staying power, like a monkey or like the wind. It ranges far, bodiless, easily changing, agitated by the objects of sense, with the six sense-fields for its sphere, connected with one thing after another.[73]

So it is impossible to identify that awareness with anything, let alone see it as 'mine'; we cannot label or name it, or any part of it. Thus we can let it be, undefined; giving up defined, bounded, and finite consciousness for the undefined and unbounded; giving up a small, tainted mind associated with suffering for a pure and open state of mind.[74]

The six-element reflection is a strong medicine, designed to cure the sickness of protective attachment to Self. It is an insight practice. It can produce a radical and lasting breakthrough into a new type of mentality, something equivalent to the arising of Bodhi mind, though the practice comes from early Buddhist systems that don't use that terminology. Nor do the poets of Europe, but sometimes they come close to the sense of liberation, as in this poem by Goethe:

> Tell a wise person, or else keep silent,
> because the mass man will mock it right away.
> I praise what is truly alive,
> what longs to be burned to death.

I Am a Miner for a Heart of Gold

In the calm water of the love-nights,
where you were begotten, where you have begotten,
a strange feeling comes over you,
when you see the silent candle burning.

Now you are no longer caught in the obsession with
     darkness,
and a desire for higher love-making sweeps you
     upward.

Distance does not make you falter.
Now, arriving in magic, flying,
and finally, insane for the light,
you are the butterfly and you are gone.
And so long as you haven't experienced this: to die and
     so to grow,
you are only a troubled guest on the dark earth.[75]

7

Mind Like the Sky

At the crossroads of the varieties of appearances and the six
*   consciousnesses,*
Is seen the confusion of the baseless phenomena of duality,
The illusory spectacles of a deceiving magician are there.
Not thinking they are true, look to their entity of emptiness,
Not letting my mind stray, may I place it within appearance
*   and emptiness.*
Making my attention unforgetful, may I maintain it within
*   appearance and emptiness.*[76]

Nāgārjuna

The rose-apple tree

The young man whose wandering forest path was to take him to
awakening and founding Buddhism had set out in a state of shock.
He had been shocked to realize that the human lot is suffering,
ageing, and death. Outrageously, he had left his wife, his baby
son, and his weeping parents to seek a solution – the deathless,
as he put it.

Finding the Mind

His first teacher told him that the goal was to be at one with infinity until no separate 'things' can be distinguished. He reached that, with an effort of will, but was not satisfied. His next teacher told him that he must somehow get beyond all perceiving, yet without destroying perception. He got that too, but it solved nothing, so he went off on his own to practise extreme austerities such as fasting and breath control. He later recalled:

> Clenching my teeth and pressing my tongue against
> the roof of my mouth, I beat down, constrained, &
> crushed my mind with my awareness.[77]

Nothing. And after six years of fruitless study and religious practice, he had almost despaired of finding the deathless. He was weak from fasting and penance, yet had the courage to realize that his self-denial wasn't working. What could he do?

There was nothing left. He was empty. Then, without warning, a vivid recollection came to him from his teenage years. One afternoon he'd been sitting under a rose-apple tree watching his father direct the annual ploughing festival. He'd felt great sympathy for the toiling labourers in the hot fields, and for their oxen, groaning under the goad. Yet as he sat there in the cool shade, no calls upon him, no anxieties, he'd felt a deep contentment. Spontaneously, his awareness had gathered and brightened, he'd never been so alive or so wide awake, yet he was profoundly calm. He basked in the stillness until the sun went down, and his father's men came searching for him.[78]

Now in the midst of his despair, some twenty years later, he could see vividly that space that his mind had once entered. And he thought to himself:

Figure 7

> Could that be the path to Awakening? ... Why am I
> afraid of that pleasure that has nothing to do with
> sensuality, nothing to do with unskilful mental
> qualities? ... I am no longer afraid ...[79]

In the joyful, natural, meditative state of mind that he recalled
from his boyhood, the future Buddha had found a sort of halfway
house to his objective of the deathless, awakening. So he sat down
in a beautiful woodland grove within earshot of a river, had a
good meal, and started meditating, exploring the path of joy.

The space of meditation

Much later, the Buddha was talking to the followers of another religion. They said: 'Surely, ultimate happiness can be gained only through self-denial and pain. Because, if one could gain happiness by doing things that one enjoys, then the King would be the enlightened one, not you, because he has much more fun than you do; after all, he can have whatever he wants.' The Buddha said: 'No, you're jumping to conclusions, assuming that possessions and power make the King happier than I am. Do you think that he could sit without moving his body or saying a word, experiencing the peak of happiness for seven days and seven nights?'[80] They didn't think he could, not even for one day. But the Buddha said that he could do this.

This is quite an extraordinary claim, don't you think, to find happiness simply through immersion in the movement and stillness of one's own mind? The Buddha was an ordinary human being, but he is said to have liberated his mind. And he is saying that one effect of this liberation is that your inner resources of happiness are like a perpetual fountain. You don't need anything from the outside to feel okay. You can just be. (In fact, the Buddha rarely sat around for days at a time just being blissed out, even though, it seems, he could have done this if he wanted to. This is because he was overwhelmingly motivated by compassion, and wanted to engage with the life of others. As far as he was concerned, the suffering of others was of no less importance than his own happiness.)

The natural thing to do when you feel a lack is to grab whatever you think you lack. But Buddhism says that it is much better to do something that completely goes against the grain – at least the first few hundred times you do it! The best thing to do is to respond to the feeling of lack by letting go. And you make sure you let go into a bigger perspective. I suppose that is the only way that works long-term, and that must have been what happened to the teenager under the rose-apple tree. This is what meditation is for: it's very hard to let go when you are in the thick of things. You need the spaciousness and lack of mental clutter of meditation in order to practise letting go.

In a meditation session, you may manage to enlarge your perspective and clear your cluttered mind; then you will enter meditative space. Your mind, your immediate experience, will start to feel different. For a start, there is the relief and simple pleasure of sitting quietly with your own experience, not needing anything else. And then there is the bliss of being absorbed in the deeper mental states, which may sometimes come in meditation, although for Buddhism blissful states of mind are not the goal of meditation practice. I'll describe these meditative states in the next section.

Then, when you get up from your meditation cushion, you find that there is temporarily an enhanced quality of quiet awareness in your life. And your awareness extends to other people as well as to your own experience – I think you will find that you can allow people to be who they are, and then even love them for who they are. On top of this, for a while you will probably experience other changes in attitude, such as increased confidence and increased creativity.

The permanent changes take much longer; they are said usually to take decades of very intensive practice. They are about radically changing your viewpoint and your habits, eventually seeing things as they really are and, as a result, developing a compassionate aspiration for enlightenment (the Bodhi mind) for the sake of everybody.

Bright and lucid mind

In principle, meditation is no more than a total involvement with some very simple experience. The only reason one thinks of sitting in a quiet place with one's eyes closed, perhaps paying attention to the breath, is that these things reduce external distraction to a minimum. Then, if your mind is neither too busy nor too sluggish, you may find that the flow of your experience becomes more and more fascinating. You become engrossed, and yet spacious, and this meditative awareness has a number of characteristics.[81]

Imagine that you are paying attention to the sensations of your breathing. First of all, your experience becomes increasingly unified. Rather than the mind jumping from one thing to another, feeling perhaps dissatisfied with what it's attending to now, you find yourself perfectly happy to stay with the breath. Consequently, any thoughts that arise will be quiet comments on the changing quality of your experience, or perhaps little reminders that keep your attention focused on the breath if you start to wander off.

What's happening is now quite fascinating, and perhaps you get excited about it. When you get completely involved (this applies outside meditation too), the experience can be thrilling. Shivers go up and down your spine, or your face flushes, or perhaps you weep. If you haven't experienced this in meditation, you might have experienced it when listening to music, or when you are really moved by a story.

In the vocabulary of Buddhism, there is one word that is sometimes translated as interest and sometimes as happiness or rapture.[82] I think this ambiguity reveals something of the nature of genuine happiness. Happiness is a feeling associated with really being involved. Even if it is difficult, it is always rewarding to be fully involved in something. This is much more satisfying and reliable than pleasure from gratifying the senses – pleasure from eating, sex, entertainment, or pleasure from personal success and approval.

If you become absorbed in meditation, really involved, you are temporarily completely contented and happy, so that there is no sense at all of any selfish need. There is nothing lacking. The odd thing is that the meditative state in its purest form feels completely ordinary. It's true that a minority of people, if they are not used to meditation, might get quite ecstatic or see visions and so forth for a while. But the straightforward contentment of sitting quietly and watching the breath – just that, nothing else – seems the way things should be all the time. Why can't we be quietly absorbed in the same way in a conversation, work, a book, our morning run, or feeding the children?

While you are being active, however, your mind is unlikely to deepen beyond the level of happy engagement, which itself is no mean feat. But in meditation, the more exciting thrill of complete involvement eventually dies down, and you get into a quiet, deep, and absorbed state. If you can stay with the process, your contentment becomes increasingly stable, so that thinking quietens completely. Then any physical thrills dissolve into the calmness, and even the happiness itself may be replaced by a profound evenness of mind. Your mind now seems vast, perhaps without perceptible boundaries.

The pool stills and clarifies

When the Buddha was describing deepening absorption in meditation, he used images of moistening and immersion. At the beginning your mind is fragmented, like bits of dried soap. But interest lubricates the mind, as if you are adding water to the lumps of soap, and with time the soap and water thoroughly mix until you have a smooth liquid – the Buddha's image for the unified mind. As the process continues, it's as if you feel more and more dissolved into the water, until you are like a mountain pool with a fresh spring welling up into it, so that it bubbles and splashes. This is the pleasure and excitement of feeling thoroughly absorbed in your meditation. But the process deepens, the excitement dies down. This is like a very deep lake with a lotus plant under the water, its every pore permeated by refreshing water, still and full of life.[83]

Table 2 Absorption of mind in meditation

Depth of absorption	Characteristics	The Buddha's image
distracted	hard to stay with the meditation, because overactive or sluggish	water disturbed by boiling, weeds, mud, coloured pollutants, or the wind
approaching absorption	the mind is stabilizing, one returns quickly from distraction, engaged with the process	[no image]
first stage of absorption	one is single-pointed, helpful thoughts, strong interest with physical thrill	soap fully moistened with water
second stage of absorption	single-pointed, thoughts have died down, interest and thrill strengthen, deeply happy	a clear pool with a deep spring welling up
third stage of absorption	single-pointed, no bodily sensations, very simple happiness	a lotus plant in a deep lake, permeated by the water

Knowing what is going on

In Buddhism, the very expanded states of mind that can open up are not the reason for meditating. Apparently there is even a risk of developing a sort of addiction to them, so you become otherworldly and passive. Instead, meditative states are a springboard to seeing what is going on, and shifting your more destructive mental habits.

Because meditative experience is simple, the stream of mental events can in principle be followed, and you can work directly on your own responses. Feeling much less self-centred you can start to see the emotional habits that feed self-centredness. You can also see the attitudes that are behind them. You've got the space to see things as they really are.

If you can hold more loosely to what arises, each of the objects of mind can be seen as inherently unstable and devoid of identity. In a profoundly calm mood, you can watch what is there without having a sense that it is crucial to yourself. Any pleasure or pain, attachment or repulsion connected with what arises is seen as impermanent and conditioned, so you can let go of it. To some extent, you can be free of identity, noticing that 'this is not mine, this is not the self'. Whatever subtle 'I-making' or 'mine-making' is still going on can be seen as inherently frustrating, and you can start to gently disentangle it like a knot in your headphone wires.

Openness

The most pure-hearted philosophers will start from the ground of their unknowing, and look as unflinchingly as possible at their experience. Thus Socrates discovered he was the wisest in Greece because he was the only one who knew he didn't know. And thus Descartes honestly (though mistakenly) thought that he had discovered that thought itself was all that could not be doubted.

A Buddhist also starts from ignorance, but has gradually developed a certain trust in the teachings of the Buddha and later masters. In particular, someone on the Buddhist path has a sense of conditioned arising, the patterns in experience that can be discerned if one looks deeply enough. So he or she looks for the networks of circumstances that have evolved into the current situation, looks for the trends that underlie his or her own interpretations of experience, and notices how situations arise and die with the factors that condition them. At the time when I first started meditating I was sometimes prone to depression. Then, to my great relief, I couldn't help noticing that depression was not a fixed or inevitable mood: it arose, and later it mysteriously passed away again. Subsequently, I started to see that factors like strain, lack of sleep, and a pessimistic inner dialogue were all precursors of depression, and factors like exercise and meditation tended to bring it to an end. However, glib explanations were not necessarily a help – I really needed a direct intuition into what was going on.

Yes, like the philosophers, cultivate the openness that lies in not knowing, seeing if you can resist the temptation to throw up all sorts of hurried conceptual structures. Then try to look behind all the conditioned trends that you have learnt about, and see the reality itself, unmediated by concepts. That reality includes the workings of the unenlightened mind, one's own mind; and seeing how it works, enlightenment begins to dawn.

Once one sees through the conditioned nature of the mind, its cyclic habits lose their potency, and one is said to enter an unconditioned mode of being, the 'open dimension'.[84] Openness is a more positive way of looking at the transcendence of self. As one moves more and more thoroughly into an open attitude, one's experience is less and less overlain by conceptual constructs. 'First there is a mountain, then there is no mountain, then there is' – this is the singer Donovan paraphrasing a Zen insight. First we think we have captured the world with our labels, then we gradually learn to drop them and see things as open, but eventually we are back with the ordinary world, nothing special, appreciated from a completely different perspective. Experience is direct, as it is; it is aesthetic rather than intellectual, and potentially imbued with a huge significance not muddied by thinking. The imagination (in its best sense) opens up, and becomes direct insight or wisdom.

Strictly speaking, this insight is not a product of meditation. But the meditation state reduces one's usual torrent of concepts to a trickle, softening one's sense of being a subject, and so bringing awareness closer and closer to the object. Gentle reflections on conditionality in this state are what allow insight to arise, according to the early versions of the Buddhist path.

Openness and compassion

Looking at yourself openly, the *idea* of a self drops away. Looking at another openly, you sense that they are not contained in their current presentation of themselves: they too are not fixed – they are open, unlimited in potential. And in a way you can recognize each other as two minds, two mysterious subjects, two centres. How can the single sphere of reality have two centres? Yet *every* subject is at its centre.

The recognition of complete openness in others is the source of compassion. You can only be irritated by someone if you take seriously their self-presentation. An awareness free of self-interest can take in others fully, as they are. It can love the life in others, as one loves the life in oneself. It can see how the self-concerned graspings of others are the direct source of their suffering, and feel an immense sympathy as it sees this. Conversely, the ordinary compassion or sympathy that we feel for others can imbue our minds with increasing openness, and thus insight.[85]

From divided awareness to complete awareness

All the time, we rely on a mind that splits the world into inner and outer. It works fairly well in allowing us to manage ordinary life. It interfaces with the world through our physical senses, and processes its input using our rational mind, making sense of it in terms of the needs of the small mind, whose mission is to protect its own soft underbelly, which it sees as a Self.

Buddhism says that it is possible gradually to shift one's reliance on to a different kind of mind, one that does not divide the world in this way. Knowledge can instead be direct, and intuitive in the most solid sense of that word. The difference between the two modes of awareness is of extraordinary importance, because the ills of the world and of each individual spring entirely (says Buddhism) from the grasping at a self that comes naturally to the divided form of awareness. If only we could make the shift![86]

Later Buddhism says that this direct form of knowledge is the mind of a Buddha, a fully enlightened mind. And it is said to have four components. One is an awareness like a perfect mirror, reflecting the whole of experience without comment or distortion. The mirror awareness emerges through the transformation of the substrate consciousness. The small mind transforms into an awareness or knowledge of complete sameness: everything and everybody is treasured as being equally valuable. The mind consciousness transforms into the discriminating awareness, a knowledge that recognizes the uniqueness and particularity of every event. The five sense consciousnesses transform themselves into the all-performing knowledge, which deftly, creatively, and compassionately engages with the world.[87]

Table 3 The transformations of the nine consciousnesses

Substrate consciousness transforms into:	awareness like a mirror
Small mind transforms into:	knowledge of sameness
Mind consciousness transforms into:	discriminating awareness
Five sense consciousnesses transform into:	all-performing knowledge
Non-dual substrate consciousness:	does not transform

Sky-like mind

To make the shift, we need to start by taking our own mind seriously, as any good Buddhist should. What do we find? The centre of our mind cannot be looked at, because it is never an object. It is that which looks, so we can't study it (except as an idea) in the way that we can study any object of experience. It is the act of being aware of an object, and Buddhism says that without an object there is never consciousness, and never a subject. So what we are really talking about is 'consciousness-of-an-object'. It is not any single fixed entity: it is momentary and constantly shifting. It is an endless stream of awarenesses of objects that themselves continually change. Each moment of consciousness arises in dependence upon its object and on preceding states of consciousness, and it moves as the object does. This means it cannot be a Self, an independent or abiding entity of any kind.

If you can be thoroughly present in the movement of the objects of your consciousness, you will see they are all inherently unstable and devoid of any identity of their own. This awareness can induce a mood of profound even-mindedness, comparatively immune to the allurements and pressures that the objects of our experience usually create. You may be able to see that a purified consciousness, with no me and no mine, is possible, just 'awaring' all the time.[88]

The Buddha said that if you can let go of the five clusters, then:

> Owing to the abandonment of passion, the support
> is cut off, and there is no base for consciousness.
> Consciousness, thus unestablished, not proliferating,
> not performing any function, is released. Owing to
> its release, it is steady. Owing to its steadiness, it is
> contented. Owing to its contentment, it is not agitated.
> Not agitated, [one] is totally unbound [awakened].[89]

But you can experience your mind as already and always unbound, in a sense, like a great blue sky. Disturbing thoughts and impulses are clouds that blow across the sky, but you don't need to leap on them and ride them until they collect into a great fog. There they are; they can pass, and new ones can come in. The vast blue sky in itself is always there above the clouds, as we see in a magical way when we fly high in a jet aircraft. Similarly our spacious mind, the fact of awareness itself, is never spoilt by the constricted thoughts that pass through it. The Buddhist vision of the mind is something like this vast blue sky.

8

The Buddha
in the Laboratory

*The rediscovery of Asian philosophy, particularly of the
Buddhist tradition, is a second Renaissance in the cultural
history of the West, with the potential to be equally
important as the rediscovery of Greek thought in the
European Renaissance.*[90]

Francisco Varela

Western traditions – dualism

We've surveyed Buddhist views of the mind in some detail. What
of modern Western views? I have left this topic until last, because
I wanted us to imbibe something of the Buddhist world-view first.

In ancient Greece, the fount of so many of our current Western
notions, Aristotle saw the mind as just one of the functions of the
human body. Ever since, Western thinkers have been preoccupied
with just how a physical matrix can give rise to personal

experience. In contrast, Aristotle's teacher, Plato, imagined human experience as being like a shadow play watched by chained men gazing into a cave. Thus we are passive spectators of a separate external world that we struggle to make sense of.

The materialism of Aristotle and the subject–object dualism of Plato colour just about all Western ideas about the mind. (It is quite hard to avoid painting Buddhism in the same hues, but this doesn't really do Buddhism justice.) Christian doctrine needed human interior life to reflect a persisting mental substance, an immortal soul. Thus Descartes in the seventeenth century felt himself compelled by the vividness of his internal experience, seen in a Christian framework, to affirm a real mental substance that runs in parallel with the physical brain, the two somehow influencing each other. You can see the problem – if the brain is absolutely not a mental thing and the mind is absolutely not a physical thing, then how can the two touch each other and interact? How could my mental decision result in phoning my mum, and how could the physical vibrations coming out of the phone let me know she needs something from the shop? Incidentally, lacking souls, animals for Descartes have no mental substance, and are merely mechanisms.

For Buddhism, the two are interdependent: one of the Buddha's disciples taught that consciousness and the sentient body are dependent upon each other, 'as if two sheaves of reeds were to stand leaning against one another.'[91] Buddhism does make various distinctions between mental and physical (as we would say) processes. However, it avoids some of the problems of dualism by rejecting the idea of substances altogether. Reality is a web of interrelated processes. All we can say is that certain things happen if the right conditions are in place, and both the effects and the conditions could be mental, could be physical, or could be a combination of the two. In the end, all we have is an ever-changing flux of experience, which we break down into particular events, mental states, observed objective things, and so on for the convenience of our understanding. But none of these things and events has any independent reality in its own right.

As Western philosophy developed, Plato's cave analogy became a 'theatre' of consciousness, all for our own entertainment, where we, the subject, sit watching the perceived world milling about on the stage. A few decades after Descartes, the English philosopher John Locke defined consciousness as 'the perception of what passes in a man's own mind.'[92] At first sight this looks quite acceptable. However, who is doing the perceiving? What does it mean for something to be 'passing' 'in' a 'mind'? (And, as with Descartes, why a 'man', as if other living creatures have no consciousness?) And is a man's mind really his 'own'?

It's hard, if not impossible, to imagine no subject–object division. An important Buddhist school sees subject and object as 'grasper' and 'grasped'. You can't conceive of a thing grasped without a grasper, nor the other way round. If we are honest, we have a simple flow of experience, which seems to have two poles or faces to it, one of which we label as interior, and the other as exterior. The exterior pole is the 'objective constituent of the perceptual situation'.[93] In the end it is said to be possible to have access to an awakened mode of awareness in which the subject–object split is no longer necessary, except perhaps for communicating with people who remain immersed in it.

Western traditions – materialism and free will

Coming up to date, in modern consciousness studies materialist ideas are dominant. They assume that reality is one substance and not two, and that this substance – matter – is made up of atoms arranged in all sorts of ordered structures interacting with each other through force fields such as gravity and electromagnetism.

Somehow, what we describe as personal experience is solely a product of these physical processes, especially in our brains.

Does this materialist view allow free will? If everything is really physical, then our impression that we make free choices that cause things to happen through our words and actions must be mistaken. The implausibility of this conclusion – that free will is illusory – is a big problem for Western philosophers.

Once again the problem does not really arise in Buddhism because the assumptions are different. In fact, the Buddha warned against allowing yourself to be dominated by preconceived assumptions or views at all. Choice is constrained by what is possible and is influenced by deep, strong urges. Nevertheless, having a genuine choice between courses of action is a common and indisputable experience, probably universal among human beings.

If you adopt the view that you *can't* genuinely choose to intervene in events, your view may influence your choices (which are still, paradoxically, experienced as free), even to the extent of teaching you to feel more constrained. Nevertheless, can this view completely destroy your sense of having some choice? Probably not. Choice remains a part of experience, a real mental event. So 'choosing' the view that you have no free will seems unproductive (since it constrains you), as well as contradicting your real experience. A 'belief' in free will (as opposed to the experience) is also a view which may influence your choices. But do you need to bother with the view? Just act! It seems in any case that, as insight into the way things really are becomes stronger, the experience of oneself as a person making willed decisions ebbs away, and spontaneous action becomes the norm.

Self and the birth of psychology

William James, the brother of the novelist Henry James, is regarded as the founder of modern psychology. His textbook on the subject was published in 1890.[94] It is scientific in approach, but what I really find stimulating about it is that it starts off by taking introspection seriously. Until recently, modern psychologists have neglected their revered founding sage in this respect, having no trust at all in introspection.[95]

James says that you should start from your actual mental states, noticing the main fact that consciousness goes on. It has four characteristics:

1. Every state tends to be part of a personal consciousness.
2. Within this, states are always changing.
3. Each state seems to be continuous.
4. Each state of consciousness chooses aspects of the apparently outside world to attend to.

So we choose: our attention is selective, rather like a torch beam that we shine around in the cluttered attic of our world, to use James's image. 'My experience is what I agree to attend to.'[96] James saw conscious attention as a genuinely causal force, and not just the effect of physical events in the brain (materialism), but he acknowledged that no evidence could decide between the two alternatives. He said that he had decided against materialism on ethical grounds.[97]

The most remarkable thing about conscious awareness, for James, is what he calls the 'great splitting of the universe into two halves ... we all draw the line of division between them in a different place ... [their] names are "me" and "not-me".'[98] One has a much greater interest in the 'me and mine' parts of the universe. He then writes about 'I' as the knower, 'me' as the self which is known by self-consciousness (the empirical self), and what one regards as 'mine', which is appropriated to the 'me'.

Like the Buddha, he emphatically rejects any possibility of there being any permanent ego, soul, or spirit in addition to the fleeting but connected states of consciousness, which are all that psychology needs. Then he says:

> The consciousness of Self involves a stream of thought, each part of which as 'I' can remember those which went before, know the things they knew, and care paramountly for certain ones among them as 'me', and appropriate to these the rest. The I ... is a thought, at each moment different from that of the last moment, but appropriating the latter, together with all which the latter calls its own ... The thoughts themselves are the thinkers.[99]

The thoughts themselves are the thinkers.

So both William James and the Buddha reject a core of selfhood, and both promote introspection. One warning, though: when you look deeply into yourself and your experience, it is often not a pretty sight. The reason for this is that you are looking at the legacy of your whole past – you are not looking at the wonderful, bright, and creative future that we all have before us, if only we can find our minds and purify them of unskilfulness.

Modern science and consciousness

Buddhism shares with science an obsession with trying to make sense of human experience, welcoming every avenue of enquiry. But it is not scientific. Science studies the world. It relishes the mind's natural tendency to absolutize an objective external world; it first solidifies that world and then explores its features. What a project! Out of it has come reliable, reproducible knowledge, as well as the marvels and horrors of technology. Once you understand how the external world works, you don't need just to observe it, you can manipulate it as well, you can put its components together in new ways. Pumps and railway engines, telephones and radios, X-ray machines and machine guns, aeroplanes and atom bombs, surveillance satellites and computers. Buddhism, in contrast, keeps its focus on human experience itself. The anguish and conflict that come out of the mistakes that human consciousness makes: how can we deal with that? How can we heal the mistakes and become happy?

I won't say that science deals with the objective world and Buddhism with the subjective, because ultimately Buddhism does not recognize that distinction. Buddhism grapples with actual experience. However, science does indeed study an objective world. Even when looking at consciousness, subjectivity itself, science has to be able, by definition, to stand outside it. It has to stare at it holding a clipboard, and take notes about what it does. The scientist prods the minds of others to see how they respond. To some extent Buddhism uses similar research methods, though the object of research is generally oneself rather than a group of student volunteers. But Buddhism is about changing the nature of experience, promoting happiness by making one more realistic and less dualistic. The happiness project is a side issue in science, though generally an important one.

The science of consciousness

Let's see what conclusions consciousness-science researchers have come to in recent decades, and whether a Buddhist understanding might shed light on them; indeed whether they may shine a light on the Buddhist project.

By the late nineteenth century, science had triumphed, or believed it had triumphed, in providing explanations for everything that happens in terms of the interactions of physical objects obeying physical laws. Some say that the last crevice to be illuminated by science is human experience itself. It may appear to be a little crevice, but it opens into the vast universe of the mind.

We know there are brain cells and sense organs, and those organs are picking something up from a world of things. Yet there is also our awareness, our conscious experience, which seems nothing like a wrinkled wet mass of scintillating cells, and it is (by definition, though definitions can be misleading) distinct from the world it seems to observe. Because science has triumphed in everything else, the unquestioned question for the modern student of consciousness is: how can 'subjective' experience arise from an objective nervous system interacting with an objective world? This question is known as the hard problem: 'The hard problem ... is the question of how physical processes in the brain give rise to subjective experience.'[100] Mind must be what brains do.

So what might the whole story be? Imagine you see an apple and then reach for it. We might say that information has reached your brain through the eye and the optic nerve, so that you had a conscious experience of an apple and made the decision to eat it, which then gave rise to nerve impulses from the brain to the arm and hand. But how can electricity in the optic nerve produce an experience of an apple? And how could a decision cause the nerves to the arm to fire? Neurophysiology seems to leave no room for the experiential side of this process.

Perhaps it would help to elaborate the picture. Thus some people build on William James' analogy of the torch beam of attention, so that the mind is like a theatre stage with a moving spotlight – whatever is in the light is 'in' consciousness.[101] Others speak of certain higher-order brain processes having the function of monitoring other brain processes to make them conscious, as if with an inner eye.[102] In both cases there is a mysterious inner observer in everybody. Who is this observer? Do they also have a mind and their own brain processes with their own inner observer again? Somehow there seems to be a problem both with consciousness as a space like a theatre in which things happen, and with the idea of an inner spectator.

Does the present happen in the past?

In the 1960s, it was common for surgeons to perform operations that required exposing a substantial part of the brain, and an American neuroscientist, Benjamin Libet, took the opportunity (with consent) to stimulate patients' brains electrically while they were awake, and ask them what they felt. He concluded that a sensation only becomes conscious if there is half a second of brain activity following the stimulation, and we then refer the experience backwards in time by half a second to compensate for the delay.[103] The present moment, it seems, happened half a second ago!

Strangely, we can show signs of recognizing something, though unaware of the fact, and even begin a physical response, *before* the half-second delay has elapsed. So it may be that sometimes we believe we have made a careful conscious decision, yet we started to respond before we were conscious even of what we were responding to.

When do we register a sensory experience? If a light flashes, surely the *experience* can't happen at precisely the moment of the flash. It takes a little time to register in the eye and then in the brain. Is it when it reaches the brain that the experience happens? If so, exactly where on the neural pathways that the signal follows does it become a conscious experience? Is it when it reaches some special consciousness centre? Is it half a second later, after some special consciousness-inducing process is complete, as Libet says?

In a test, first a light flashes as a command to move. Around a fifth of a second later, the experimenter can pick up brain responses setting up the right signals to the muscles to respond physically. However, the subject reports that he or she made the decision later – after half a second or so. Nevertheless, it is still possible for the subject to change their mind and veto the action, so free will is not compromised by these experiments.[104]

The experiments do seem to show that you can't exactly place conscious experiences in time. Maybe it's impossible to say that an experience either was or was not 'in consciousness' at a particular moment of time, indeed consciousness is not literally a space 'in' which experiences happen, that is just a metaphor. Is the world in the mind? Is the mind in the world?[105] In any case, the subjects were being asked to report something some time after the experience, and maybe there was a process of making sense of what happened that prevented a proper recall of the bare experience. Would skilled meditators recount these things differently?

We tend to think of time as an inexorable conveyor belt that carries us along at a steady rate. But studies of consciousness, whether via the brain or via deep personal experience, disturbingly challenge this idea of time. We all know how a week's holiday can seem over in a flash and an hour at the dentist seems like a whole day (meditation practice highlights the subjectivity of time experience).[106] It is less well known that if a sound comes after a flash of light, say, it's quite easy to think that the sound came first.[107] So experience and a camcorder may disagree about the timing, the duration, and even the order of events.

What about dreams, do they happen in real time? In 1861, Alfred Maury (a French doctor) remembered a long, involved dream of being led off to the guillotine. Its narrative seemed to have been created to make sense of part of his bed falling onto his neck, which woke him up, so he proposed that dreams are concocted upon waking.[108] But correlations between the duration of REM (rapid eye movement, which usually accompanies reported dreaming) and the length of dreams, as well as earlier external stimulation influencing a dream, show that dreams take about the same time as visualizing the same events awake, and so (it is concluded) can't be formulated at the moment of awakening.

On the other hand, the philosopher Daniel Dennett presents various theories reconciling the memories you get upon waking up with the idea that dreams are not really being experienced at the time.[109] The sleeper will always say 'I experienced it', because that is what memory says, but this does not prove that dreams are 'in consciousness'. Thus, perhaps, in REM sleep many brain processes occur, and a thread is concocted on waking from the confusing memories of them, though many such stories were possible. This is rather similar to a Buddhist teacher's suggestion, based on his own experience, that dreams are constructed on the basis of a sequence of recalled emotions; more than one narrative could have fitted the sequence of emotions, but one involuntarily drops into one particular narrative, which then seems a memory of the real dream.[110]

Making sense of mind

Consciousness studies are in a fertile and rather chaotic period. Theories jostle for prominence as new results come in from brain studies and even from studies of Buddhist meditators. So rather than trying to summarize all the theories, I'll sketch out some ideas from Daniel Dennett, the dream theorist of the last paragraph. He is one of the most prominent philosophers in the field. Dennett applies a robust scepticism both to common-sense notions of the mind and to theories inherited from Western philosophical and religious traditions, concluding that we are conscious, but the phenomena of consciousness as we tend to describe them are illusory. His own predisposition (we all have one) is for a materialist standpoint arising from the belief that mental structures must arise in the same process of Darwinian evolution that produced the bodies that house them.

Dennett rejects the theatre analogy: 'neither the show nor the audience is to be found in the brain ... the only real place there is to look for them'.[111]
Instead, he considers the multitude of processes going on in the brain, some being perceptions initiated through the senses, and others being thoughts, all constantly revised as they interact with each other, like the many drafts of a novel that the author is struggling to complete satisfactorily.[112] No Self is having these experiences; they are not really shown in any theatre; there is no place they arrive into in order to become conscious.

However, sometimes a story does reach the light of day. This is because we sometimes 'probe' the drafts, perhaps by asking a question of ourselves. So a narrative emerges from the stream of consciousness, which affects behaviour, and is repeatedly revised. Both experiences and the narrative (which is another experience) leave traces in the memory that are accessed later and affect later narratives, leaving their own memory traces to overlay and perhaps alter the previous ones.

> Mental contents become conscious not by entering
> some special chamber in the brain, not by being
> transduced into some privileged and mysterious
> medium, but by winning the competitions against
> other mental contents for domination in the control
> of behaviour, and hence for achieving long-lasting
> effects – or as we misleadingly say, 'entering into
> memory.' And since we are talkers, and since talking to

ourselves is one of our most influential activities, one
of the most effective ways ... for a mental content to
become influential is for it to get into position to drive
the language-using parts of the controls. All this has to
happen in the arena of the brain ... but not under the
direction of anything.[113]

There are no discoverable 'facts' about which contents were
or were not conscious at any one time. But because we have a
narrative, we also have a benign illusion of a self, the author of
the story, a story which arises from how the streams of processes
are probed.

For example, we may suddenly conclude that we were unaware
of our driving for the past ten minutes. We feel certain that we
weren't 'there' in that period, but all we can know (says Dennett)
is that none of the probing (if any) that happened during those
ten minutes left any traces in memory.[114] The probing produces
a stream of silent talking to ourselves, trying to make sense of
experience, which fixes the contents, and leads to how we describe
them later. Whenever we probe, we recall memories that may
become part of the story. We cannot catch ourselves *not* being
conscious (as you can't open the fridge door and catch the light
being off), and our probing, our enquiry, concocts a traceable path
through the events we find in memory by paying attention to
them, so there is an apparently unified self having a unified thread
of experience.

So what is *actually* going on is a turbulent river of electro-
chemical processes in the brain; out of it emerge both experience
and experiencer, says Dennett. We have a strong drive to make
sense of our experience, so the gaps and inconsistencies that might
interrupt the continuity of thoughts and perceptions tend to be
edited out as we draft and redraft our story.

> Our tales ... spin us. Our human consciousness, and our
> narrative selfhood, is their product, not their source.[115]

We think we have a privileged access to our inner states, which
indeed we do, but the access is to how it *seems*, and our accounts
of observations are really impromptu theorizing, creating stories
about our inner lives. The science of consciousness is dealing with
the stories: only measured brain states can be regarded as facts.

I want to leave this quite cogent theory without too much
comment, except to notice that meditation seems to show the
possibility of being conscious without any probing going on,
though our later description of the experience does indeed rely on
probing into memory and then verbalizing it. Like any description
of mental processes, Dennett's relies on metaphor – drafting and
redrafting a story is a powerful image that helps to envisage
mental processes without a real controlling Self. Having seen
through the illusion, Dennett feels that there is no more explaining
to do, and it is fine to stop there. However, we still have the fact
of awareness. What could it mean to conclude, as he does, that
that fact is simply delusional?

The Buddhist position is that our accounts are indeed
largely delusional. Nevertheless, the subtle glow of awareness
can genuinely illuminate the river of experience, and training
(or perhaps a sudden radical shift of viewpoint) can increase
the intensity and continuity of that illumination. Potentially,
awareness is a direct presence in experience rather than a story
being told about it. For Dennett, awareness is only apparent, and
the only mental facts that need explaining are how it 'seems'.
Buddhist insight claims to inhabit how it actually is. Could that
be possible?

A new stance on the mind

An increasing number of consciousness researchers have studied the Buddhist approach, and some make use of meditation. Consequently, the results of neuroscience and of Buddhist insight are being compared, and there are signs of an exciting synthesis emerging. At the forefront was the Chilean neuroscientist and Buddhist Francisco Varela, who helped the Dalai Lama to launch his very fruitful biennial 'Mind and life' conferences.[116] Varela died tragically young in 2001, but many of his colleagues are still trying to catch up with his profound conclusions.

He incorporated careful brain experiments into his view, but took human experience and accounts of experience very seriously indeed, insisting that studying the interaction between inextricable mind and world is essential for understanding consciousness:

> Cognition is not the representation of a pregiven world by a pregiven mind but rather the enactment of a world and a mind on the basis of a history of the variety of actions that a being in the world performs.[117]

Introspection helps us understand our minds, but only if it is genuinely mindful, which means being fully 'embodied', as well as open-ended. It is not reflection *on* experience, it is experience itself, taking us closer to reality than the abstract and disembodied 'view from nowhere' of Western philosophy.[118] Understanding one's mind through mindfulness requires training, learning to master both one's mind and one's body. It also requires courage, because sooner or later in the ever-shifting dance of experience one finds 'no one at home',[119] the reality of egolessness. This is quite disturbing, and one's mind tends to pull away from it by fabricating a lasting, separate, and independent ego where there is none, the classic Buddhist experience of unsatisfactoriness. Yet, says Varela, being empty of Self is the same thing as being filled with experience: an inviolable Self requires debarring anything that might affect it, so only dropping that illusion allows us to relish the riches of life, marrying the inner and outer worlds.

Studies of cognition back up these Buddhist conclusions. For example, colour categories are not the projection of a pregiven inner world, nor do they merely recover a pregiven outer world. They, like other forms of cognition, come from an active physical engagement with the world. Perception is a form of action, it is not passive; it solves the problem of how to guide one's action in specific local situations that constantly change as a result of one's activity.

Without an ego-self, we have no ground to stand on in ourselves as subject, and there is no objective stable ground outside either. There is just a world that extends beyond us, but can't be found apart from our bodies, language, and social history, so that 'knower and known, mind and world, stand in relation to each other through mutual specification'.[120] Thus reality beyond the duality of inner and outer is simply openness, śūnyatā.

It seems to me that Buddhism and the scientific approach are already becoming close allies as we try to come to grips with our experience as human beings, the play of our minds. Another cognitive scientist sympathetic to Buddhism describes the contribution that each can make:

> Whereas the Buddhist scholars have an enormous descriptive understanding of consciousness, viewed from the internal perspective and addressing complex aspects of mind, complete with a framework for defining what questions are important and what classifications are most useful, neuroscience has none of these things. Indeed, it has largely avoided issues of consciousness, introspection and complex

mental phenomena altogether. Conversely, while science libraries in the West are filled with objective, extrospective data on the minute details of the mechanisms underlying different functions of the brain, as well as its microscopic anatomy, the Buddhists have almost completely ignored both the question of the mechanisms of mind and the understanding that can be gained by detailed external observations.[121]

Conclusion

The mind is not a vessel that needs filling, but wood that needs igniting.[122]

Plutarch

Stop and realize

I genuinely felt hesitant about producing a book of this nature. Does it just add to the fog of ideas that obscure the simple awareness that we are left with if we can stop being so mentally busy? Certainly, it's best to start by attending, dropping preconceptions as far as possible. Buddhist meditation means attending persistently to your experience. Its phases are sometimes called 'stop and realize' – cease the anxious chatter of explanation and evaluation, and realize what is actually going on.

Attending to experience, we may start to notice, in a peaceful clarity, that our world of events impinges upon us from all sides like a cascade of confetti at a huge wedding. And we notice that we have always assumed there is something in the middle – our Self. But when we try to go outside and observe the Self, like the shepherd boy and the monk Ānanda, we find we have no success. The mind itself will not be picked up and looked at.

Yet awareness is there, experience is happening.

Buddhism explains the mind

It is so hard to explain who we are, and what is going on. We don't need to explain it, we can just live. However, life is not straightforward: it keeps presenting us with problems and even anguish as we realize that there are so many things we hold dear, yet they slip away, or we never possess them. So when Buddhism supplies explanations, it is not so much for the purpose of satisfying curiosity, as for the purpose of tackling the frustrations of this unsatisfactory human life, and setting the scene for the liberation of the mind from its self-centredness.

One explanation is the substrate model of chapter 2. Hidden in the depths of our minds is a fertile terrain in which the seeds of our actions lie dormant, or sprout into new experiences. The small mind fences off a little patch of this landscape as its own garden, defending it from perceived threats, augmenting it with treasures furtively grabbed from over the fence. It believes that it has established a hermetic selfhood, which is the garden in the substrate. That selfhood must be the agent, receiving news, making decisions, vowing to resist the besieging world forever. Its spies are the six sense consciousnesses.

Yet there is nothing stable in our inner experience: whatever we are is intertwined with the stream of events, and dances with that stream. All we can find, says early Buddhism, is five clusters: bodily form, felt responses, perceivings/recognizings, impulses, and conscious awareness itself. We tend to look within these clusters for something to identify with, clutching at it, and responding with dismay when it alters.

The model of the clusters turned out to be too ponderous for later Buddhist psychology, and was superseded by a number of detailed catalogues of possible mental events and functions.[123] But the clusters do clarify how perception happens, as a sensory impression sparks off feeling responses and the recognition process, which enter consciousness and set off an avalanche of impulses and karmic actions. It is even said that the impulses, those seeds in the substrate, have such a strong momentum that they persist after the death of the body, and influence the development and personality of a baby beginning a future life.

The kind of lives available to us, and the impulses that motivate them, are illustrated in the wheel of life, a mirror of self-awareness, described in chapter 3. The outer rim of the mirror shows how ignorant consciousness, attached to a fictitious Self, tumbles through a sequence of linked states, producing frustration and loss and entrenching the ignorance. The turning of the wheel seems inexorable, but awareness of the process shows that there are points at which we can intervene and slow its movement, even reverse its direction. We need to become vividly aware of our habit energies, and how some of them are destructive and harmful. These unskilful habits are amenable to restraint; what is more, they can be replaced by skilful habits. Instead of being governed by our personal legacy of preferences, we can use skilful and unskilful as the criteria for how we live, and so gradually unstick from anxious self-clinging.

It's as if a mind whose image is the wheel of life transmutes into a mind whose image is the shining jewel held in Buddhist art by the Bodhisattva of compassion. This jewel is the Bodhi mind, which is set both on the freedom of awakening and on the open compassion that is its emotional counterpart. Defensive separateness from others is based on an illusion, and solidarity with others is much wiser as well as being kinder.

Advancement in wisdom can be symbolized by the multilevel Buddhist stūpa. Its first storey represents the earth element and, as we add more storeys – and elements – one by one, we are building a structure of progressive liberation, culminating in an open consciousness situated in an open spaciousness.

The liberation of one's mind is impelled by a sense of all that is wrong in one's own life and in the world. Yet all the steps of liberation, from the beginning, are tinged with joy. The mind absorbed in meditation is particularly suffused with peaceful happiness, and absorbed states are quiet enough for echoes of the truth to be heard, clear enough for one to begin to see how things fit together, and find the mind. When the mind is genuinely realistic and insightful, it is also compassionate. At last free of anxious self-protection, one can take a deep interest in others.

So we've encountered some Buddhist theoretical structures that attempt to explain the mind, a few of the lists so beloved by Indian thinkers. But I hope I have also conveyed the practical emphasis of Buddhism: just be there in your experience, and attend to it – what do you notice?

Inevitably we come to Buddhism with our own preconceptions, many of them unconscious ones derived from our immersion in Western culture. For this reason I wanted to provide a number of connections with Western ideas of the mind, including examples of Western thinkers coming to similar conclusions to Buddhism. Buddhism has no monopoly on insight into the truth, and the greatest Western poets and thinkers have often, at least to some extent, arrived at the same insights, generally with no input from the Buddhist tradition.

Taming the bull

Finding the mind is an adventure, a scramble through the forests of human experience. I learnt meditation as a student in Brighton, and I used to sit in my little room with my eyes closed trying to

Figure 8

stay with my breaths, five of them, six of them, and then I'd find
myself thinking about something extraneous again. I would open
my eyes and see the Buddha. My father had given me a beautiful
bronze Burmese statue of the Buddha, which he had found in the
Portobello Road market in London, a few hundred metres from
where I am writing this now. I felt I could see a kindly serenity
and a profound happiness in the Buddha's face, and I closed my
eyes, and started again trying to find my mind. I am still looking
for it, and trying to stay with it when I find it.

The elusive and untamed mind appears as a wild bull in what
you could call a classic graphic novel of Chinese Zen Buddhism
– ten scenes depicted over and over by the greatest artists. In
the third frame, a lost boy glimpses the tail of the bull through
the trees. He patiently tracks the animal; it gets used to him and

eventually permits him to ride it back into the village. Then the two of them, now close friends, vanish into the mountains, and the picture simply shows a brush-drawn loop, representing the timeless unity of the boy and the bull, the bull of his mind. But the loop is not the last picture. In the final frame, the boy returns to the marketplace: he's now a jovial adult 'with bliss-bestowing hands'. The bull is nowhere to be seen.[124]

The Buddhist project is seeking the mind, taming it, even letting it go, until in exhaustion we realize there is nothing to be found, and there is nothing to stop an exuberance of compassionate activity.

Notes

1 Yūhō Yokoi, *Zen Master Dōgen: An Introduction with Selected Writings*, Weatherhill, New York 1987, p.56.

2 *The Connected Discourses of the Buddha*, translated by Bhikkhu Bodhi, Wisdom, Boston 2000, p.603. The analogy should not be taken too literally; the Buddha did not believe that our ruined minds were once awakened.

3 'Looking' here is meant in the sense of genuinely becoming more receptive to what is going on. Charlotte Joko Beck, *Nothing Special: Living Zen*, HarperCollins, New York 1995, p.151.

4 Laura Riding, 'In Laddery Street Herself', from *Forgotten Girlhood*, in *The Rattle Bag*, ed. S. Heaney and T. Hughes, Faber & Faber, London 1982, p.162.

5 St Augustine, *Confessions*, book 10, chapter 8, quoted in *Waving: Webster's Quotations, Facts and Phrases*, Icon Group International, San Diego, CA 2009, p.1.

6 Einstein, recounted by Herbert Feigl in his *The 'Mental' and the 'Physical'*, University of Minnesota Press, Minneapolis 1967, p.138. Feigl translates euphemistically 'dirt' for 'shit'.

7 G.C. Chang, *The Hundred Thousand Songs of Milarepa*, Shambala, Boulder, CO 1977, p.123ff.

8 What follows is paraphrased from *The Śūraṅgama Sūtra*, translated by Charles Luk, Rider, London 1966, chapter 1. In 1856, Richard Wagner planned an opera (*Die Sieger*) based on another version of this story (see www.monsalvat.no/sieger. htm, accessed 26 November 2010), and the great Bengali poet Rabindranath Tagore used it for his play *Chandalika* (1933).

9 Arthur Deikman, '"I"=Awareness', *Journal of Consciousness Studies*, 3:4 (1996), pp.350–6 (p.350).

10 G.P. Malalasekera, *Dictionary of Pali Proper Names*, 2 vols, Pali Text Society, London 1938, vol.1, p.262.

11 Robert Kaplan, *The Nothing That Is: A Natural History of Zero*, Penguin, London 1999, p.192.

12 *Aṅguttara Nikāya*, 3.33, translated by Ven. Thanissaro.

13 Thich Nhat Hanh, *Understanding Our Mind*, Parallax Press, Berkeley, CA 2006, p.25. On the *ālaya* as substrate, see Herbert Guenther, 'Basic Features of Buddhist Psychology', in *The Authority of Experience: Essays on Buddhism and Psychology*, ed. John Pickering, Curzon Press, Richmond 1997, p.82. *Ālaya* is also described as a storehouse: the substrate 'becomes the storage and clearinghouse of all the accumulated products of mentation and action since beginningless time' (*Laṅkāvatāra Sūtra*, in *A Buddhist Bible*, ed. Dwight Goddard, Dutton, New York 1938, p.306).

14 This is a term popular in Zen Buddhism, found in 'Affirming faith in mind' by the Chinese patriarch Sengcan (quoted in *Rochester Zen Center's Chant Book*, Rochester Zen Center, Rochester, NY 1990, pp.16–22). Remember that small mind is just us, responding in a particular way.

15 Sangharakshita, *Know Your Mind*, Windhorse Publications, Birmingham 1998, p.52. Note that the subjective pole is also not completely under one's control.

16 *Laṅkāvatāra Sūtra*, p.303. My line divisions.

17 Sangharakshita, *Know Your Mind*, p.56.

18 Peter Harvey, *The Selfless Mind*, Curzon Press, London 1995, p.40.

19 *Udāna*, 32, quoted in Harvey, *The Selfless Mind*, p.41.

20 The five skandhas (Pali: *khandhas*), often translated as 'heaps' or 'aggregates'.

21 *Saṃyuttanikāya*, 22.1, translated by Ven. Thanissaro.

22 This allegory is from the *Aṭṭhasālini*, quoted in Harvey, *The Selfless Mind*, p.147, adapted to make it easier to follow.

23 *The Tibetan Book of the Dead*, translated by Robert Thurman, Bantam, New York 1993.

24 Nagapriya, *Exploring Karma and Rebirth*, Windhorse Publications, Birmingham 2004, p.36.

25 James Joyce, *Ulysses*, 9.1044–6.

26 Goethe, *Wilhelm Meister*, translated by Robert Carlyle, Collier, New York 1962, pp.454–5.

27 Sangharakshita, *The Symbolism of the Tibetan Wheel of Life*, available from www.freebuddhistaudio.com/audio/details?num=103, accessed 26 November 2010; text version from *Creative Symbols of Tantric Buddhism*, Windhorse Publications, Birmingham 2002.

28 Bertrand Russell, *Human Knowledge: Its Scope and Limits*, Allen & Unwin, London 1948, part 2, chapter 1.

29 Based on the three-minute breathing space in Mark Williams, John Teasdale, Zindel Segal, and Jon Kabat-Zinn, *The Mindful Way through Depression: Freeing Yourself from Chronic Unhappiness*, Guilford Press, London 2007, p.183.

30 For instance see Maitreyabandhu, *Life with Full Attention*, Windhorse Publications, Cambridge 2010.

31 *Dhammapada*, verse 37, my translation.

32 See chapter 8.

33 The substrate, *ālaya*, is not a part of early Buddhist psychology, but there is an equivalent called the *bhavaṅga*. See Harvey, *The Selfless Mind*, p.176.

34 Kulananda, *The Wheel of Life*, Windhorse Publications, Birmingham 2000. Often there are six realms (Sanskrit: *gati*) rather than five (though five is the earlier division), with the fighting gods being distinguished from the serene and peaceful ones. The illustration at the beginning of the chapter shows these two at top and upper right. Traditionally, the realms can be seen as psychological states as well as the more usual actual places of rebirth.

35 See Robin Cooper, *The Evolving Mind: Buddhism, Biology, and Consciousness*, Windhorse Publications, Birmingham 1996.

36 *Majjhima-Nikāya*, 2.32, quoted in T.W. Rhys Davids, *Pali–English Dictionary*, Pali Text Society, Chipstead 1921–5, p.394.

37 Cooper, *The Evolving Mind*, pp.212–21.

38 Some scholars conclude that the extension of conditionality to the 'objective' world was due to teachers after the time of the Buddha. See Sue Hamilton, *Early Buddhism: A New Approach*, Curzon Press, Richmond 2000.

39 Sanskrit *vijñāna* is usually translated as 'consciousness'. It is another word for 'mind' (*citta*); *vijñāna* is used when looking at the knowing function of mind, awareness. *Citta* is usually the more general term, the 'inner' environment of all mental processes.

40 The early texts always list the links as a chain starting with ignorance and ending with ageing and death. The wheel of life image joins up the beginning and end into a circle, and indeed the Buddha in early texts often talks about the circularity of the world of ordinary experience. Unfortunately, we do tend to respond to suffering and the ending of things with a retrenched mistaken view of life (for example, 'I am a helpless victim'), which impels us around the circle again.

41 *Majjhima-Nikāya*, 1.263. The 'sentient body' for the fourth link is Peter Harvey's translation of *nāma-rūpa*, literally 'name-and-form' (*The Selfless Mind*, p.117).

42 Rilke, *Letters to a Young Poet*, translated by M.D. Herter, Norton, New York 1954, p.76.

43 Lawrence Durrell, *Tunc*, Faber, London 1968, p.271.

44 George Eliot, *Romola*, Penguin, Harmondsworth 1980, p.151.

45 *Majjhima Nikāya*, 3.36. Also see *Saṃyutta Nikāya*, 3.101 and 4.202.

46 Definition of mine-making (*mamaṅkāra*) in the *Pali–English Dictionary*, p.523.

47 A.A. Milne, *Winnie the Pooh*, Methuen, London 1926, p.33ff.

48 The root of frustration (1) in craving (2), the prospect (3) of eradicating the root, and the methods (4) for doing so make up the four noble truths, a central and characteristic teaching of the Buddha.

49 There is more on this period in the Buddha's life in chapter 7.

50 Sangharakshita, *Know Your Mind*, pp.162–241.

51 *Saṃyutta Nikāya*, 15.8, in *The Connected Discourses of the Buddha*, p.958.

52 Kenneth White, from 'Walking the coast', in *The Bird Path*, Mainstream, Edinburgh 1989, p.58.

53 Sanskrit: Bodhicitta. This term is particularly associated with the Mahayana Buddhist schools, not with early Buddhism. Early Buddhism has the similar concept of freedom-mind (*cetovimutti*), strongly associated with the practice of universal-friendliness meditation. See for example *Aṅguttara Nikāya*, 11.16, and also the next chapter.

54 *Aṅguttara Nikāya*, 1.6.2.

55 The mantra *oṃ maṇi padme hūṃ* is popularly thought to refer to a jewel (*maṇi*) in a lotus (*padma*), though in fact it contains no indication of 'in'.

56 *Majjhima Nikāya*, 26.

57 The substrate model includes its own special explanation of how this transition happens – see chapter 7.

58 Buddhaghosa, *Visuddhimagga*, translated by Bhikkhu Ñāṇamoli as *The Path of Purification*, Buddhist Publication Society, Kandy 1991, chapter 9, which describes the stages of the meditation. Also see Vessantara, *The Heart*, Windhorse Publications, Birmingham 2006.

59 See Vessantara, *The Heart*.

60 Śāntideva, *A Guide to the Bodhisattva Way of Life*, translated by V.A. and B.A. Wallace, Snow Lion Publications, Ithaca, NY 1997, p.27 (stanzas 89–96).

61 You need to have defined some boundaries before you can dissolve them. Some people can get caught up in other people's crises to the extent that they forget their own needs, and so cause more harm than good in the long run.

62 *Buddhist Wisdom Books*, translated by Edward Conze, Unwin, London 1988, p.25.

63 Gampopa, *The Jewel Ornament of Liberation*, Lion Publications, Ithaca NY 1998, p.130.

64 Ralph Waldo Emerson, journal entry, 20 May 1831 (*The Journals and Miscellaneous Notebooks*, Harvard University Press, Cambridge, MA 1963, p.255).

65 Yuanwu (twelfth century?), quoted on the e-sangha internet forum, 31 May 2004.

66 Dōgen , from the *Genjōkōan*, translator untraced.

67 *The Udāna*, translated by John D. Ireland, Buddhist Publication Society, Kandy 1997, p.74.

68 This book is about the mind rather than Buddhist ethics, so I won't list the precepts here, but see Sangharakshita, *Living Ethically: Advice from Nagarjuna's Precious Garland*, Windhorse Publications, Cambridge 2009.

69 Liberation of consciousness (Pali: *cetovimutti*) and liberation through wisdom (Pali: *paññāvimutti*); see for instance *Aṅguttara Nikāya*, 6.13 and 9.44.

70 Lama Govinda, *Psycho-Cosmic Symbolism of the Buddhist Stupa*, Dharma Publishing, Emeryville, CA 1976, p.66.

71 Herbert Guenther, *Philosophy and Psychology in the Abhidharma*, Random House, London 1957, pp.144–63; Sangharakshita, *Creative Symbols of Tantric Buddhism*, p.40.

72 *Majjhima Nikāya*, 62.

73 *Ratnacūḍa Sūtra*, quoted in Śāntideva's *Śikṣāsamuccaya*, translated by Conze, in *Buddhist Texts Through the Ages*, Cassirer, Oxford 1954, p.163, abridged by Thich Nhat Hanh. The term for 'mind' here is *citta*, for which Conze uses 'thought' – I have changed this in the quoted extract.

74 Sangharakshita, *What Is the Dharma?*, Windhorse Publications, Birmingham 1998, pp.196–7; *The Middle Length Discourses of the Buddha*, translated by Bhikkhu Ñāṇamoli and Bhikkhu Bodhi, Wisdom Publications, Boston 1995, p.1091; Kamalashila, *Meditation: The Buddhist Way of Tranquillity and Insight*, Windhorse Publications, Birmingham 1992, p.211.

75 Goethe, 'The holy longing' (1814), translated by Robert Bly, in *The Rag and Bone Shop of the Heart*, HarperCollins, New York 1993, p.282.

76 Nāgārjuna, 'The song of the four mindfulnesses', in *The Precious Garland*, translated by Jeffrey Hopkins, Harper & Row, New York 1975, p.118. Nāgārjuna is referring to professional magicians, who would perform at major junctions in ancient India, making things appear and disappear for the amazement of the crowds. Similarly, appearances enter our consciousness, and we take them as solid; they do genuinely appear, but like the tricks of a conjuror they are empty of self nature – see the 'Openness' section in this chapter.

77 *Majjhima Nikāya*, 36, translated by Ven. Thanissaro.

78 Described in Aśvaghoṣa's *Buddhacarita*, translated by Edward Conze, in *Buddhist Scriptures*, Penguin, Harmondsworth 1959, p.42.

79 *Majjhima Nikāya*, 36, translated by Ven. Thanissaro.

80 *Majjhima Nikāya*, 1.95, paraphrased.

81 See Kamalashila, *Meditation*, pp.66–73. The Buddhist descriptions of consciousness would seem to take you as far as the human mind can possibly go. For this reason, much of what is in this chapter is not something that I can relate from my own experience. It's what my teachers and the traditional accounts seem to be trying to put across.

82 Sanskrit: *prīti*; Pali: *pīti*.

83 See Kamalashila, *Meditation*, pp.66–74. There are further stages, deeper than the three in Table 2. The Buddha's images for the different kinds of distraction (water boiling, weedy, and so on) are from *Saṃyutta Nikāya*, 5.121–4.

84 Herbert Guenther, *Kindly Bent to Ease Us*, part 1, Dharma Publishing, Emeryville, CA 1975, pp.169 and 264. Also see his *Tibetan Buddhism in Western Perspective*, Dharma Publishing, Emeryville, CA 1977, pp.73–4. The 'open dimension' is Guenther's translation of the Sanskrit *śūnyatā*, often translated as 'emptiness'.

85 I owe many of the reflections in this and the previous paragraph to Subhuti, from a 1996 seminar I attended with him.

86 In Sanskrit the two modes of consciousness are respectively *vijñāna* (can be etymologized as 'divided knowing') and *jñāna*. See Sangharakshita, lecture on *Wisdom Beyond Words*, available from http://www.freebuddhistaudio.com/audio/details?num=179, accessed 27 November 2010.

87 The transformation of the eight consciousnesses (*vijñānas*) into the five knowledges (*jñānas*) is crucial to the Yogacāra analysis of the Buddhist path. Vessantara, in *Meeting the Buddhas* (Windhorse Publications, Birmingham 1993, chapters 5 to 10, and table on p.52), goes into these transformations, and the way they connect to the mythical five Buddhas of the mandala in Vajrayāna Buddhism.

88 I am indebted for many of the points in this and the previous paragraph to oral teachings on consciousness as the sixth element by Subhuti.

89 *Saṃyutta Nikāya*, 22.53, translated by Ven. Thanissaro.

90 Francisco Varela, Evan Thompson, and Eleanor Rosch, *The Embodied Mind*, MIT Press, Cambridge, MA 1991, p.22.

91 *Saṃyutta Nikāya*, 12.67, translated by Ven. Thanissaro.

92 John Locke, *An Essay Concerning Human Understanding*, vol.1, Dover, New York 1959, p.138.

93 Guenther, *Philosophy and Psychology in the Abhidharma*, p.173.

94 William James, *The Principles of Psychology*, 2 vols, Macmillan, London 1890.

95 In contrast to psychologists, psychotherapists have focused strongly on introspected 'subjective' experience, their own and their patients', but under a cloud of suspicion generated by more scientifically oriented psychologists.

96 James, *The Principles of Psychology*, vol.1, p.402.

97 William James, *Pragmatism*, Harvard University Press, Cambridge, MA 1975, p.55.

98 William James, *Psychology: The Briefer Course*, University of Notre Dame Press, Indiana 1985 (first edition 1892), p.165.

99 James, *Psychology: The Briefer Course*, p.138.

100 David Chalmers, 'The Puzzle of Conscious Experience', *Scientific American*, December 1995, p.63.

101 Bernard Baars, *A Cognitive Theory of Consciousness*, Cambridge University Press, Cambridge 1988, p.31. Note that the 'theatre' idea is not from William James.

102 Susan Blackmore, *Consciousness: An Introduction*, Hodder & Stoughton, London 2003, p.47.

103 See Jeffrey M. Schwartz and S. Begley, *The Mind and the Brain: Neuroplasticity and the Power of Mental Force*, HarperCollins, New York 2002, pp.303–5.

104 See Schwartz and Begley, *The Mind and the Brain*, pp.307–10.

105 Experience seems to happen in an illuminated 'space', but you can't say cogently that the space is internal, nor that it is external.

106 Sangharakshita, *The Three Jewels*, 4th edition, Windhorse Publications, Birmingham 1998, p.60. Sangharakshita here explains the tradition that the meditative absorptions are equivalent to purely mental realms of existence, in which time is enormously prolonged. He suggests that 'since ultimately it is consciousness that determines both space- and time-perception, and since the entire phenomenal universe exists nowhere save in space and time, it is evident not only that consciousness determines being but that in essence being is consciousness' (quoting the first verse of the *Dhammapada* as source).

107 Blackmore, *Consciousness: An Introduction*, p.61.

108 Inge Strauch and Barbara Meier, *In Search of Dreams: Results of Experimental Dream Research*, State University of New York Press, Albany, NY 1996, p.11.

109 Blackmore, *Consciousness: An Introduction*, pp.346–7.

110 Sangharakshita, personal verbal communication and transcribed seminar, 'The Forest Monks of Sri Lanka', part 3, available from http://www.freebuddhistaudio.com/texts/seminartexts/SEM065P3_Forest_Monks_of_Sri_Lanka_-_Part_3.pdf, p.4, accessed 2 August 2010.

111 Daniel Dennett, *Consciousness Explained*, Little Brown, and Co., Boston 1991, p.134.

112 Dennett's 'multiple drafts model', in *Consciousness Explained*, p.111ff.

113 Daniel Dennett, *Freedom Evolves*, Viking, New York 2003, p.254.

114 Dennett, *Consciousness Explained*, p.137.

115 Dennett, *Consciousness Explained*, p.418.

116 Their 1987 genesis is described by the Dalai Lama in *The Universe in a Single Atom*, Little, Brown, and Co., London 2005, p.38.

117 Varela, Thompson, and Rosch, *The Embodied Mind*, p.9. For simplicity, I ascribe the conclusions described in this book just to the first author, Varela.

118 Nagel, quoted in Varela, Thompson, and Rosch, *The Embodied Mind*, p.25.

119 Varela, Thompson, and Rosch, *The Embodied Mind*, p.61.

120 Varela, Thompson, and Rosch, *The Embodied Mind*, p.149. Also see p.217ff.

121 Christopher deCharms, *Two Views of Mind: Abhidharma and Brain Science*, Snow Lion Publications, Ithaca, NY 1997, p.228.

122 Plutarch, 'On Listening to Lectures', available from http://en.wikiquote.org/wiki/Plutarch, accessed 2 August 2010.

123 Known as the Abhidharma; see Sangharakshita, *Know Your Mind*.

124 The images are the so-called ox-herding pictures. See, for instance, Philip Kapleau, *The Three Pillars of Zen*, Rider, London 1980, pp.313–25.

Recommended Reading

Robin Cooper, *The Evolving Mind: Buddhism, Biology, and Consciousness*. A Buddhist angle on how consciousness may have evolved: Windhorse Publications, Birmingham 1996.

The Dhammapada (many translations are available). The Buddha's own sayings on the mind and the Buddhist path.

Peter Harvey, *The Selfless Mind*. A thorough scholarly account of the early Buddhist approach to mind and no-self: Curzon Press, London 1995.

Kamalashila, *Buddhist Meditation: Tranquillity, Imagination and Insight*. Buddhist meditation practices and the ideas behind them: Windhorse Publications, Cambridge 2012.

Kulananda, *Principles of Buddhism*. A quick guide to Buddhism as a whole: Windhorse Publications, Birmingham 2004.

Sangharakshita, *Know Your Mind*. A Western Buddhist commentary on Buddhist views of the mind: Windhorse Publications, Birmingham 1998.

Francisco Varela, Evan Thompson, and Eleanor Rosch, *The Embodied Mind*. Cognitive science and human experience from a combined neuroscience, philosophical, and Buddhist point of view: MIT Press, Cambridge, MA 1991.

Acknowledgements

Many, many thanks to the following people for comments on this book in its various stages of formation, and for personal teachings that have enhanced my own understanding of the Buddhist Dharma: Advayachitta, Jnanasiddhi, Priyananda, Shaun Bhattacherjee, Mahabodhi, Dhatvisvari, Claudine Edwards, Saraha, Jayarava, Ratnaguna, Subhuti, Urgyen Sangharakshita.

Index

air element, 80
ālaya, 24
all-performing knowledge, 98
Ānanda, 14
animals
  and reflexive consciousness, 45
  as conscious, 39
  as mechanisms, 102
Aristotle, 101
asceticism, 60
attention, selective, 105
Augustine, 11
Avalokiteśvara, 66
aversion, 58
awakening, and bodhi mind, 68
awareness, 10
  as radiant, 68
  degrees of, 44
  four enlightened, 98
  illuminating experience, 114
  need for practice, 17

Beck, Charlotte Joko, 6
Bodhi mind, 66
  and Śāntideva, 70
bodhicitta, 129
Bodhisattva, of compassion, 66
body, 30
brain, 102, 108, 112
breaking down the barriers, 69

Buddha
  and Ānanda, 14
  his quest, 87
  image, 65
  images for meditation, 93
  mind of, 98
  mind poem, 43
  on wheel of life, 51
  rose-apple tree meditation, 88
Buddhism
  and happiness project, 107
  and science, 106, 116
  as evolutionary, 46
  teachings and personal quest, 23
Buddhist ethics, 59
bull (ox-herding pictures), 123

cetovimutti, 130
child
  and rebirth, 36
  describing experience, 9
  self-awareness in, 12
citta, 128
city, forgotten, 2
clusters, clinging, 30
colour categories, 116
comparison, 29
compassion
  activity, 66
  and openness, 97

Index

compassion (*cont.*)
  and wisdom, 72
  goddess of, 19
conceit, I am, 56
conditioned arising, 47
  and meditation, 95
consciousness
  and time, 109, 134
  and William James, 105
  as a cluster, 30
  as an element, 82
  as divided knowing, 48
  as momentary, 82
  evolution of, 46
  mental, 26
  multiple drafts theory, 112
  needs an object, 27
  reflexive, 39
  science of, 107
  sense, 26
  tainted thinking, 24
  theatre of, 103, 108, 112
  with no me or mine, 99
consciousnesses
  eight or nine, 26
  transform into awarenesses, 98
craving, 58

Dalai Lama, 115
Daniel Dennett, 111
death, and rebirth, 34
deathless, 87
Deikman, Arthur, 17
Descartes, 95, 102
Diamond Sūtra, 72
discriminating awareness, 98
Dōgen, 1, 75
Donovan, 96
dreams, 110
dualism, subject-object, 116
Durrell, Lawrence, 55

earth element, 79
Einstein, 11

elements
  and stūpa, 79
  six, reflecting on, 81
Eliot, George, 55
Emerson, 73
emotion, veil of, 68
emptiness and appearance, 87
enactment of world and mind, 115
enlightened mind, 98
ethics, Buddhist, 43, 76
evolution of consciousness, 46
experience
  attending to, 4
  illuminated, 11
  inside and outside, 5
  present, 11, 21
explorer finding city, 2

feelings, 30
fire element, 79
free will, 104, 110
freedom, taste of, 76
Freud, Sigmund, 44
friendliness meditation, 69

gem, 67
God, not in Buddhism, 46
Goethe, 37, 84
Guanyin, 19, 66

habits, 54
  skilful, 76
happiness
  from engagement, 60
  through meditation, 90
hard problem, 108
harm, from unskilfulness, 60
hedonism, 60

I
  and I am conceit, 56
  and I-making, 56, 63
  and William James, 105
  as the observer, 18
  I am conceit, 29
  just an idea, 29

identity, 57
ignorance, 25, 53
impulses, 30
insecurity, 56
insight, 96, 114
insight reflection, 84
integration and the stūpa, 80
introspection, 17, 115
  in William James, 105

James, William, 105
Japan, stūpa gravestones, 79
jewel net, 74
jñāna, 132
Joyce, James, 37

Kaplan, Robert, 23
karma, 34
  and seeds, 24
  not the only causation, 36

lack, 90
Laṅkāvatāra Sūtra, 28
liberation, through friendliness and
    wisdom, 77
Libet, Benjamin, 109
likes and dislikes, 58
links, twelve, 47
listening, inner, 20
Locke, John, 103
lotus, 67

mantra, of compassion, 67
materialism
  and Daniel Dennett, 112
  and rebirth, 36
  and William James, 105
  in consciousness studies, 103
  of Aristotle, 102
Maury, Alfred, 110
meditation, 4
  absorption, 92
  and awareness, 114
  as ordinary, 93
  Buddha's boyhood, 88

meditation (*cont.*)
  Buddha's images, 93
  Buddhist, 20
  letting go, 91
  method for Ānanda, 19
  on friendliness, 69
  radical insight and compassion, 91
  rapture, 92
  seeing things as really are, 95
  stop and realize, 119
memory, and consciousness, 112
Milarepa, 12
Milne, A.A., 58
mind
  and matter, 27
  as restricted, 83
  central in Buddhism, 3
  embodied, 115
  like sky, 100
  location of, 15
  needs an object, 83
  observing, 14
  small, 24
Mind and life conferences, 115
mind-body dualism, 102
mindfulness
  noticing habits, 59
  of breathing, 42
  three minute exercise, 41
  total, 40
  training, 115
mine-making, 56, 63
mirror
  and wheel of life, 39
  awareness, 98
mirror exercise, 50
monkey, on wheel of life, 51

Nāgārjuna, 87

objective world, 27
openness, 96
opposites as water, 79

Index

pagoda, 77
pain, deters from awareness, 40
paññāvimutti, 130
perception, 14
    as a cluster, 30
    as a process, 31
    as action, 116
    inner and outer, 26
personality, without identifying, 63
Plato, 102
pleasure and meditation, 89
Plutarch, 119
possessions, 57
preferences, 57
prison, and stūpa, 79
psychology, Buddhist and Western,
    44
psychotherapy, 133

realms, wheel of life, 46
rebirth, 34
resistance and the elements, 81
Riding, Laura, 9
Rilke, 53
Russell, Bertrand, 39

sameness awareness, 98
Śāntideva, 70
science
    and Buddhism, 106
    of consciousness, 107
seeds, as acts, 24
self
    and WIlliam James, 106
    as illusion, 113
    empty of (Varela), 116
    fixed view, 29
    hungry, 61
    independent, 29
self, non-, 99
self-awareness, and wheel of life, 39

selfish attachment, 57
selfishness, 55
senses, 26
shepherd boy, 12
skilful and unskilful, 59, 62
Socrates, 95
soul, Christian, 102
space element, 80
spontaneity, 76, 104
stūpa, 77
subject and object
    as grasper and grasped, 103
    dualism, 102
substances rejected by Buddhism,
    102
substrate, 24
suffering, 75
    from unskilfulness, 60
śūnyatā, 116
Śūraṅgama Sūtra, 14
sympathy, and compassion, 72

Theseus, ship of, 23
thinking, 18
Tibetan Book of the Dead, 35

unconscious, 45
unskilful mental states, 61

Varela, Francisco, 101, 115
veils, emotional and cognitive, 68
views, 68, 104
vijñāna, 48, 128, 132

water element, 79
wheel of life, 39
White, Kenneth, 65
wisdom, 96
    and compassion, 72

Yogacāra, 132

WINDHORSE PUBLICATIONS

Windhorse Publications is a Buddhist charitable company based in the UK. We place great emphasis on producing books of high quality that are accessible and relevant to those interested in Buddhism at whatever level. We are the main publisher of the works of Sangharakshita, the founder of the Triratna Buddhist Order and Community. Our books draw on the whole range of the Buddhist tradition, including translations of traditional texts, commentaries, books that make links with contemporary culture and ways of life, biographies of Buddhists, and works on meditation.

As a not-for-profit enterprise, we ensure that all surplus income is invested in new books and improved production methods, to better communicate Buddhism in the 21st Century. We welcome donations to help us continue our work - to find out more, go to www.windhorsepublications.com.

The Windhorse is a mythical animal that flies over the earth carrying on its back three precious jewels, bringing these invaluable gifts to all humanity: the Buddha (the 'awakened one') his teaching, and the community of all his followers.

Windhorse Publications
169 Mill Road
Cambridge CB1 3AN
UK
info@windhorsepublications.com

Perseus Distribution
1094 Flex Drive
Jackson TN 38301
USA

Windhorse Books
PO Box 574
Newtown NSW 2042
Australia

THE TRIRATNA BUDDHIST COMMUNITY

Windhorse Publications is a part of the Triratna Buddhist Community, which has more than sixty centres on five continents. Through these centres, members of the Triratna Buddhist Order offer classes in meditation and Buddhism, from an introductory to deeper levels of commitment. Bodywork classes such as yoga, Tai chi, and massage are also taught at many Triratna centres. Members of the Triratna community run retreat centres around the world, and the Karuna Trust, a UK fundraising charity that supports social welfare projects in the slums and villages of South Asia.

Many Triratna centres have residential spiritual communities and ethical Right Livelihood businesses associated with them. Arts activities are encouraged too, as is the development of strong bonds of friendship between people who share the same ideals. In this way Triratna is developing a unique approach to Buddhism, not simply as a set of techniques, but as a creatively directed way of life for people living in the modern world.

If you would like more information about Triratna please visit www.thebuddhistcentre.com or write to:

London Buddhist Centre
51 Roman Road
London E2 0HU
UK

Aryaloka
14 Heartwood Circle
Newmarket NH 03857
USA

Sydney Buddhist Centre
24 Enmore Road
Sydney NSW 2042
Australia

Also from Windhorse Publications

Solitude and Loneliness: A Buddhist View
by Sarvananda

Charlie Chaplin observed, 'Loneliness is the theme of everyone.' Although true, it is equally true that we all very skillfully, and often unconsciously, organize our lives in such a way as to avoid loneliness.

Drawing on a wide range of sources – the poets Dickinson and Hafiz, the painter Edward Hopper, the sage Milarepa, the lives of Helen Keller and Chris McCandless, and of course the Buddha – Sarvananda explores the themes of isolation, loneliness and solitude from a Buddhist perspective and examines how and why our relationship to ourselves can be a source of both suffering and liberation.

ISBN 9781 907314 07 0
£8.99 / $13.95 / €10.95
152 pages

Meditating: A Buddhist View
by Jinananda

Meditation is a household word, everyone has their idea of what it is, but does this mean that it is more misunderstood than understood? Here Jinananda, an experienced meditation teacher, gives us the Buddhist perspective. He shows us that – far from being a safe, patching-up, therapeutic tool – meditation is a radical, transformative, waking-up practice.

Buddhist meditation is about being true to your experience, and this means getting behind the idea of what is going on, behind the label, to the ungraspable experience of this moment. Jinananda shows you how to start doing this, how to sit comfortably for meditation, and how to do two meditation practices that develop clarity, peace of mind and positive emotions.

ISBN 9781 9073140 6 3
£8.99 / $13.95 / €10.95
160 pages

Saving the Earth: A Buddhist View
by Akuppa

If you been wondering how to make a difference in protecting the environment but didn't know where to start, this guide is the solution. Filled with practical tips as well as insightful reflections, *Saving the Earth* provides tools for change while showing how the Buddhist philosophies of interconnectedness and compassion are of immense use in our efforts towards preserving the Earth.

ISBN 9781 899579 99 0
£7.99 / $13.95 / €9.95
144 pages

Vegetarianism: A Buddhist View
by Bodhipaksa

How does what we eat affect us and our world? Is there a connection between vegetarianism and living a spiritual life? Doesn't HH the Dalai Lama eat meat?

A trained vet, respected teacher and happy vegan, Bodhipaksa answers all of these questions and more. Tackling issues such as genetically modified vegetables and modern ways of producing food he dispels widespread myths and reflects upon the diets dominant in the contemporary West. In comparison, he considers the diets of wandering monks in Ancient India and the diet of the Buddha himself.

By considering why people eat meat and relating this to Buddhist ethics he explores habits and the possibility of change. He takes a positive view of the benefits of vegetarianism, and shows practically, how to maintain a healthy and balanced vegan or vegetarian lifestyle.

This exploration shows how a meat-free life can not only lighten the body but also the soul.

ISBN 9781 899579 96 9
£7.99 / $13.95 / €9.95
104 pages

Meaning in Life: A Buddhist View
by Sarvananda

How can we bring more sense of significance into our lives? What meaning does life have in the face of suffering or death? Do we have a 'why' to live for?

Sarvananda draws a parallel between the Buddha's quest and our own search for meaning in the modern world. Using references from the 20th century, he covers many of the ways in which we seek meaning, citing writers and thinkers such as Akira Kurosawa, Wordsworth and Woody Allen. In so doing he moves from individual understanding to the principles of Buddhist teaching and demonstrates in a calm, friendly way how to apply the teachings practically, before finally taking the reader to a deeper reality.

A concise, witty exploration of what truly matters.

ISBN 9781 899579 87 7
£7.99 / $13.95 / €9.95
144 pages

Buddhism: Tools for Living Your Life
by Vajragupta

In this guide for all those seeking a meaningful spiritual path, Vajragupta provides clear explanations of the main Buddhist teachings, as well as a variety of exercises designed to help readers develop or deepen their practice.

Appealing, readable, and practical, blending accessible teachings, practices, and personal stories . . . as directly relevant to modern life as it is comprehensive and rigorous. – Tricycle: The Buddhist Review, 2007

I'm very pleased that someone has finally written this book! At last, a real 'toolkit' for living a Buddhist life, his practical suggestions are hard to resist! – Saddhanandi, Chair of Taraloka Retreat Centre

ISBN 9781 899579 74 7
£10.99 / $16.95 / €16.95
192 pages

A Path for Parents
by Sara Burns

A Path for Parents is for anyone interested in spiritual life within the context of parenting. Sara Burns, mother and Buddhist practitioner, draws on her own experience to deliver a refreshingly honest and accessible account of how parents can grow spiritually among their everyday experiences of life with children.

ISBN 9781 899579 70 9
£11.99 / $17.95 / €17.95
176 pages

A Guide to the Buddhist Path
by Sangharakshita

The Buddhist tradition, with its numerous schools and teachings, can understandably feel daunting. Which teachings really matter? How can one begin to practise Buddhism in a systematic way? This can be confusing territory. Without a guide one can easily get dispirited or lost.

Profoundly experienced in Buddhist practice, intimately familiar with its main schools, and founder of the Triratna Buddhist Community, Sangharakshita is the ideal guide. In this highly readable anthology he sorts out fact from myth and theory from practice to reveal the principal ideals and teachings of Buddhism. The result is a reliable and far-reaching guide to this inspiring path.

ISBN 9781 907314 05 6
£16.99 / $23.95 / €19.95
264 pages

The Buddha's Noble Eightfold Path
by Sangharakshita

The Noble Eightfold Path is the most widely known of the Buddha's teachings. It is ancient, extending back to the Buddha's first discourse and is highly valued as a unique treasury of wisdom and practical guidance on how to live our lives.

This introduction takes the reader deeper while always remaining practical, inspiring and accessible. Sangharakshita translates ancient teachings and makes them relevant to the way we live our lives today.

Probably the best 'life coaching' manual you'll ever read, the key to living with clarity and awareness. – Karen Robinson, *The Sunday Times*

ISBN 9781 899579 81 5
£9.99 / $16.95 / €16.95
176 pages